Cute & Cozy
STASHBUSTERS

BY KNIT PICKS

Photography by Amy Setter

Printed in the United States of America

First Printing, 2018

ISBN 978-1-62767-210-8

Versa Press, Inc

800-447-7829

www.versapress.com

CONTENTS

CHEVRON HAT AND MITTS

by Tori Gurbisz

FINISHED MEASUREMENTS

Hat: 18 (20.25, 22.25)" circumference x 11 (11.25, 11.75)" tall.

Mitts: 6.25 (7, 7.75)" circumference x 8.25" tall.

YARN

Hat:

Knit Picks Andean Treasure
(100% Baby Alpaca; 110 yards/50g): C1 Fog Heather 23490, C2 Calypso Heather 26566, 2 balls each.

Mitts:

Knit Picks Andean Treasure
(100% Baby Alpaca; 110 yards/50g): C1 Fog Heather 23490, C2 Calypso Heather 26566, 1 ball each.

NEEDLES

US 5 (3.75mm) DPNs or circular needles, or size to obtain gauge.

US 4 (3.5mm) DPNs or circular needles, or one size smaller than size to obtain gauge.

NOTIONS

Yarn Needle
Stitch Markers
Scrap Yarn or Stitch Holder
Large Pom-pom Maker (optional)

GAUGE

23 sts and 30 rows = 4" in St st and Chevron Pattern in the round on larger needles, blocked.

Notes:

The Chevron Hat and Mitts are both worked from the bottom up in the round. Slip stitch chevrons create a stranded look, but there is only one color used per round. This project is great for playing with color combinations, and more than two colors may be used to make those small bits of leftover yarn go even farther.

When working charts in the rnd, read each row from right to left, as a RS row.

Stockinette Stitch (St st, in the rnd over any number of sts)
All Rnds: K.

Chevron Pattern (in the rnd over a multiple of 4 of sts)
Rnd 1: With C1, *Sl 3, K1; rep from * to end.
Rnd 2: With C1, *K1, Sl 1, K2; rep from * to end.
Rnds 3 and 4: With C1, K.
Rnds 5 and 6: With C2, rep Rnds 1 and 2.
Rnds 7 - 10: With C2, K.
Rnds 11 and 12: With C1, rep Rnds 1 and 2.
Rnds 13 - 16: With C1, K.
Rnds 17 and 18: With C2, rep Rnds 1 and 2.
Rnds 19 and 20: With C2, K.
Rnds 21 and 22: With C1, rep Rnds 1 and 2.

K2, P2 Rib (in the rnd over a multiple of 4 of sts)
All Rnds: * K2, P2; rep from * to end.

DIRECTIONS

Hat
The hat is worked from the bottom up in the rnd.

Brim
With C2 and smaller needle loosely CO 104 (116, 128) sts, PM and join for working in the rnd being careful not to twist sts. Work in K2, P2 Rib for 16 rnds or until piece measures 2" from CO edge.

Body
With C2 and larger needle, work in St st for 16 rnds. Work Rnds 1-22 of Chevron Pattern. Break C2; the remainder of the hat will be worked in C1.
Work in St st for 4 rnds.

Crown Shaping
Set Up Rnd: *K26 (29, 32), PM; rep from * to last 26 (29, 32) sts, K to end.
Dec Rnd: *K to 3 sts before M, CDD; rep from * to end, 8 sts dec.

Next Rnd: K.

Rep last two rnds until 2 (3, 2) sts remain between each M. 8 (12, 8) sts total.

Break yarn, leaving a tail 6-8" long. With yarn needle, thread yarn through sts and pull tight to secure top of hat.

Mitts (make 2 the same)

The mitts are worked from the bottom up in the rnd.

Cuffs

With C2 and smaller needle loosely CO 36 (40, 44) sts, PM and join for working in the rnd being careful not to twist sts. Work in K2, P2 Rib for 16 rnds or until piece measures 2" from CO edge. Switch to larger needle and work 4 rnds in St st.

Work 6 (4, 2) rnds of Chevron Pattern.

Thumb Gusset, Size 6.25" Only

If desired, the Thumb Gusset may be worked by using the chart between the beginning of rnd and Gusset M placed below.

Rnd 1: With C2 and maintaining Chevron Pattern, K1, M1L, PM for end of gusset, K1, M1L, work in established Chevron Pattern to end, 1 gusset st inc, 2 total inc.

Rnds 2 and 4: With C2, K.

Rnd 3: With C2, M1R, K2, M1L, SM, work in established Chevron Pattern to end, 2 sts inc.

Rnd 5: With C1 M1R, with C2 Sl 3, with C1 K1, M1L, SM, work in established Chevron Pattern to end, 2 sts inc.

Rnd 6: With C1, K2, with C2, Sl 1, with C1 K3, SM, work in established Chevron Pattern to end.

Rnd 7: With C1, M1R, K6, M1L, SM, work in established Chevron Pattern to end, 2 sts inc.

Rnds 8 and 10: With C1, K.

Rnd 9: With C1, M1R, K8, M1L, SM, work in established Chevron Pattern to end, 2 sts inc.

Rnd 11: With C2 M1R, with C1 Sl 2, (with C2 K1, with C1 Sl 3) twice, with C2 M1L, SM, work in established Chevron Pattern to end, 2 sts inc.

Rnd 12: With C2 K1, (with MC Sl 1, with C2 K3) twice, with C1 Sl 1, with C2 K2, SM, work in established Chevron Pattern to end.

Rnd 13: With C2, M1R, K12, M1L, SM, work in established Chevron Pattern to end, 2 sts inc.

Rnd 14: With C2, K.

Place the 14 Thumb Gusset sts between Ms on stitch holder or scrap yarn. 36 sts.

Thumb Gusset, Size 7" Only

If desired, the Thumb Gusset may be worked by using the chart between the beginning of rnd and Gusset M placed below.

Rnd 1: With C2 and maintaining Chevron Pattern, M1R, with C1 Sl 1, PM for end of gusset, M1L, Sl 2, K1, work in established Chevron pattern to end. 1 gusset st inc, 2 total inc.

Rnds 2, 4, 6: With C2, K.

Rnd 3: With C2 M1R, K2, M1L, SM, work in established Chevron Pattern to end, 2 sts inc.

Rnd 5: With C2 M1R, K4, M1L, SM, work in established Chevron Pattern to end, 2 sts inc.

Rnd 7: With C1 M1R, with C2 Sl 2, with C1 K1, with C2 Sl 3, with C1 M1L, SM, work in established Chevron Pattern to end, 2 sts inc.

Rnd 8: With C1 K1, with C2 Sl 1, with C1 K3, with C2 Sl 1, with C1 K2, SM, work in established Chevron Pattern to end.

Rnd 9: With C1 M1R, K8, M1L, SM, work in established Chevron Pattern to end, 2 sts inc.

Rnds 10 and 12: With C1, K.

Rnd 11: With C1 M1R, K10, M1L, SM, work in established Chevron Pattern to end, 2 sts inc.

Rnd 13: With C2 M1R, With C1 Sl 1, (with C2 K1, with C1 Sl 3) twice, with C2 K1, with C1 Sl 2, With C2 M1L, SM, work in established Chevron Pattern to end, 2 sts inc.

Rnd 14: With C2 K4, (with C1 SL 1, with C2 K3) twice, with C1 Sl 1, with C2 K1, SM, work in established Chevron Pattern to end.

Rnd 15: With C2 M1R, K14, M1L, SM, work in established Chevron Pattern to end, 2 sts inc.

Rnd 16: With C2, K.

Place the 16 Thumb Gusset sts between Ms on stitch holder or scrap yarn. 40 sts.

Thumb Gusset, Size 7.75" Only

If desired, the Thumb Gusset may be worked by using the chart between the beginning of rnd and Gusset M placed below.

Rnd 1: With C1, maintaining Chevron Pattern, K1, M1L, PM for end of gusset, K1, M1L, work in established Chevron Pattern to end. 1 gusset st inc, 2 total inc.

Rnd 2: With C1, K.

Rnd 3: With C2 M1R, with C1 Sl 2, with C2 M1L, SM, work in established Chevron Pattern to end, 2 sts inc.

Rnd 4: With C2 K1, with C1 Sl 1, with C2 K2, SM, work in established Chevron Pattern to end

Rnd 5: With C2 M1R, K4, M1L, SM, work in established Chevron Pattern to end, 2 sts inc.

Rnds 6 and 8: With C2, K.

Rnd 7: With C2 M1R, K6, M1L, SM, work in established Chevron Pattern to end, 2 sts inc.

Rnd 9: With C1 M1R, with C2 Sl 1, with C1 K1, with C2 Sl 3, with C1 K1, with C2 Sl 2, with C1 M1L, SM, work in established Chevron Pattern to end, 2 sts inc.

Rnd 10: With C1 K4, with C2 Sl 1, with C1 K3, with C2 Sl 1, with C1 K1, SM, work in established Chevron Pattern to end.

Rnd 11: With C1 M1R, K10, M1L, SM, work in established Chevron Pattern to end, 2 sts inc.

Rnds 12 and 14 : With C1, K.

Rnd 13: With C1 M1R, K12, M1L, SM, work in established Chevron Pattern to end, 2 sts inc.

Rnd 15: With C2 M1R, (with C2 K1, with C1 Sl 3) 3 times, with C2 K1, with C1 Sl 1, with C2 M1L, SM, work in established Chevron Pattern to end, 2 sts inc.

Rnd 16: (With C2 K3, with C1 Sl 1) 3 times, with C2 K4, SM, work in established Chevron Pattern to end.

Rnd 17: With C2 M1R, K16, M1L, SM, work in established Chevron Pattern to end, 2 sts inc.

Rnd 18: With C2, K.

Place the 18 Thumb Gusset sts between Ms on stitch holder or scrap yarn. 44 sts.

Hand

Work last 2 rnds of Chevron Pattern. With C1, work 12 rnds in St st. Switch to smaller needle, work 8 rnds in K2, P2 Rib. Loosely BO in Rib.

Thumb

Place held thumb sts on larger needle, with C2 work 8 rnds in St st. Loosely BO all sts.

Finishing, Hat and Mitts

Weave in ends, wash and block to finished measurements. If desired, with C1 and large Pom-pom maker, make pom-pom, secure to top of Hat.

Legend

☐ **K**
Knit stitch

Ⅴ **Slip Stitch (sl)**
Slip stitch as if to purl with yarn in back.

Ⅿ **Make One Left**
Pick up the bar between stitch just worked and the next stitch on needle, inserting LH needle from front to back; purl through the backloop.

Make One Right
MR Pick up the bar between stitch just worked and the next stitch on needle, inserting LH needle from back to front; knit through the front loop.

☐ C1

■ C2

■ No Stitch

Chevron Pattern Chart

4	3	2	1	
		V		22
	V	V	V	21
				20
				19
		V		18
	V	V	V	17
				16
				15
				14
				13
		V		12
	V	V	V	11
				10
				9
		V		8
	V	V	V	7
				6
				5
				4
				3
		V		2
	V	V	V	1

Thumb Gusset Chart 6.25"

14	13	12	11	10	9	8	7	6	5	4	3	2	1	
														14
ML												MR		13
					V		V				V			12
		ML	V	V	V		V	V	V		V	MR		11
														10
			ML								MR			9
														8
				ML					MR					7
							V							6
					ML	V	V	V	MR					5
														4
					ML			MR						3
														2
						ML								1

Thumb Gusset Chart 7″

16	15	14	13	12	11	10	9	8	7	6	5	4	3	2	1	
																16
ML														MR		15
		V				V				V						14
	ML	V	V		V	V	V		V	V	V		V	MR		13
																12
		ML										MR				11
																10
			ML								MR					9
						V			V							8
				ML	V	V		V	V	MR						7
																6
					ML				MR							5
																4
						ML		MR								3
																2
							V	MR								1

Thumb Gusset Chart 7.75″

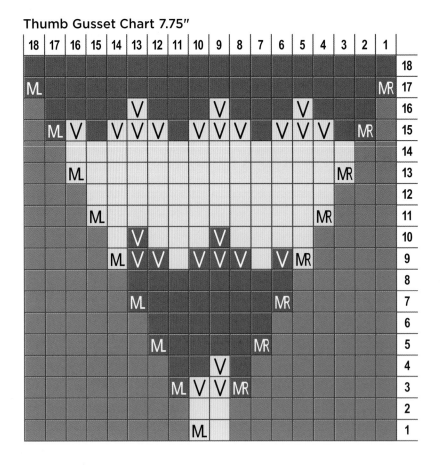

18	17	16	15	14	13	12	11	10	9	8	7	6	5	4	3	2	1	
																		18
ML																MR		17
					V				V				V					16
		ML	V		V	V	V		V	V	V		V	V		MR		15
																		14
			ML												MR			13
																		12
				ML									MR					11
					V				V									10
				ML	V	V		V	V	V		V	MR					9
																		8
					ML						MR							7
																		6
						ML				MR								5
									V									4
							ML	V	V	MR								3
																		2
								ML										1

CONFETTI REIGNS COWL

by Kathe Christensen

FINISHED MEASUREMENTS
10.5" high x 24.75" circumference.

YARN

Knit Picks Stroll Sock Yarn
(75% Fine Superwash Merino Wool, 25% Nylon; 231 yards/50 g): C1 White 26082, C2 Dove Heather 25023, C3 Hollyberry 27234, 1 ball each.

NEEDLES
US 5 (3.75mm) 24" circular needle, or size to obtain gauge.

NOTIONS
Yarn Needle
Stitch Markers

GAUGE
28 sts and 32 rows = 4" over Confetti Reigns Stitch Pattern in the rnd, blocked.

Notes:

The Confetti Reigns Cowl is a short cowl designed to incorporate three colors into a stranded knit project. If using three different colors, choose one light, one medium and one darker shade. It works very well using individual colors or a monochromatic color change. Two-colored 1x1 Ribbing is used to edge this cowl.

The Confetti Reigns stitch chart is knit using the stranded knitting technique of catching long floats (yarn carried behind work) every three stitches. When working the chart, read each row from right to left as a RS row.

DIRECTIONS

With C1 loosely CO 164 sts. Join in the rnd, being careful not to twist sts. PM for the beginning of the rnd.
*With C1, K1; with C2, P1; rep from * to end of rnd.
Next Rnd: With C1 K all sts, increasing 10 sts evenly spaced: *K15, M1, K16, M1; rep from * to last 9 sts, K9. – 174 sts.
Begin Confetti Reigns Stitch Chart
The chart is worked in the rnd and all sts are knit. Work Rnds 1 through 24 a total of 3 times.
Next Rnd: With C1, K all sts, decreasing 10 sts evenly spaced: *K2tog every 15 sts; rep from * to last 4 sts, K4 – 164 sts.
Next 3 Rnds, 1x1 Rib: *With C1, K1; with C3, P1; rep from *. Work one rnd of ribbing as established with C1.

Finishing

With Color C1, BO loosely, weave in ends and block.

Legend

- ☐ K — Knit stitch
- ☐ C1
- ▨ C2
- ▦ C3

Confetti Reigns Stitch Chart

6	5	4	3	2	1	
C1	C1	C1	C3	C1	C1	24
C1	C3	C3	C1	C3	C3	23
C3	C3	C1	C1	C1	C1	22
C1	C3	C3	C1	C1	C1	21
C1	C1	C3	C1	C1	C3	20
C1	C3	C3	C3	C3	C3	19
C3	C3	C3	C3	C3	C3	18
C3	C3	C3	C3	C3	C3	17
C3	C3	C3	C2	C3	C3	16
C3	C2	C2	C3	C3	C3	15
C2	C2	C3	C3	C3	C2	14
C3	C2	C2	C3	C2	C2	13
C3	C3	C2	C2	C2	C3	12
C3	C2	C2	C2	C2	C2	11
C2	C2	C2	C2	C2	C2	10
C2	C2	C2	C2	C2	C2	9
C2	C2	C2	C1	C2	C2	8
C2	C1	C1	C2	C2	C2	7
C1	C1	C2	C2	C2	C2	6
C2	C1	C1	C1	C2	C2	5
C2	C2	C1	C1	C1	C2	4
C2	C1	C1	C1	C1	C1	3
C1	C1	C1	C1	C1	C1	2
C1	C1	C1	C1	C1	C1	1

DOTS DOTS DOTS HAT

by Emily O'Brien

FINISHED MEASUREMENTS
16.5 (19.75, 23.25)" circumference x 9.5 (10, 10.5)" high.

YARN
Knit Picks Palette
(100% Peruvian Highland Wool; 231 yards/50g): MC Black 23729, C1 Chicory 24577, C2 Cyan 24583, C3 Peapod 25098, C4 Canary 25531, C5 Orange 24554, C6 Serrano 24553; 1 ball each (all colors aside from MC can be 5g scraps)

NEEDLES
US 2 (3mm) 16" circular needle or DPNs, or one size smaller than size to obtain gauge.

US 3 (3.25mm) DPNs or one 32" or longer circular needle for Magic Loop technique, or size to obtain gauge.

NOTIONS
Yarn Needle
Stitch Markers
Pompom Maker

GAUGE
29 sts and 39 rows = 4" in stranded St st in the round, blocked.

Notes:

Go stash diving and make a mini colorwork fade! This simple hat is a great way to use up small scraps of yarn and have fun with color. Plus, who doesn't love a multicolor pompom? The hat is worked bottom up in the round starting with a brim of twisted ribbing. Stranded colorwork creates stripes of dots. The whole thing is topped off with a colorful pompom.

Read each row of the chart from right to left as a RS row, knitting all sts.

Twisted Rib (in the rnd over an even number of sts)
All Rnds: (K1TBL, P) to end.

Dots Dots Dots Pattern (in the rnd over an even number of sts)
Rnd 1: *K1 in CC, K1 in MC; rep from * to end of rnd.
Rnd 2: K in MC.
Rep Rnds 1-2 for pattern.

DIRECTIONS
Using smaller needle, loosely CO 120 (144, 168) sts. Join to work in rnd being careful not to twist sts, and place beginning of rnd marker if desired.

Brim
Work in Twisted Rib for .75 (1, 1.25)".

Head
Switch to larger needle. Knit 4 rnds.
Then move onto Colorwork.

Colorwork
Work Dots Dots Dots pattern with C1 as CC.
Work Dots Dots Dots pattern with C2 as CC.
Work Dots Dots Dots pattern with C3 as CC.
Work Dots Dots Dots pattern with C4 as CC.
Work Dots Dots Dots pattern with C5 as CC.
Work Dots Dots Dots pattern with C6 as CC.
Work Dots Dots Dots pattern with C5 as CC.
Work Dots Dots Dots pattern with C4 as CC.
Work Dots Dots Dots pattern with C3 as CC.
Work Dots Dots Dots pattern with C2 as CC.
Work Dots Dots Dots pattern with C1 as CC.

Crown Set Up
K in MC until hat is 6 (6.5, 7)" long.
Next Rnd: (K24, PM) around.

Crown Decreases
Rnd 1: (K to 2 sts before M, K2tog, SM) to end. 5 (6, 7) sts dec.
Rnd 2: Knit.
Rep Rnd 1 and Rnd 2 until there are 12 sts between each M.
Rep Rnd 1 until there is 1 st between each M. Remove M on last rnd.

Finishing
Cut yarn, leaving a 12" tail. Pull tail through remaining sts and pull tight to fasten off. Weave in all ends. Block to Finished Measurements.

Create a matching pompom by holding all of your contrasting colors at once and wrapping them around a pompom maker as if they are one yarn. This will give you a pompom with even color distribution.

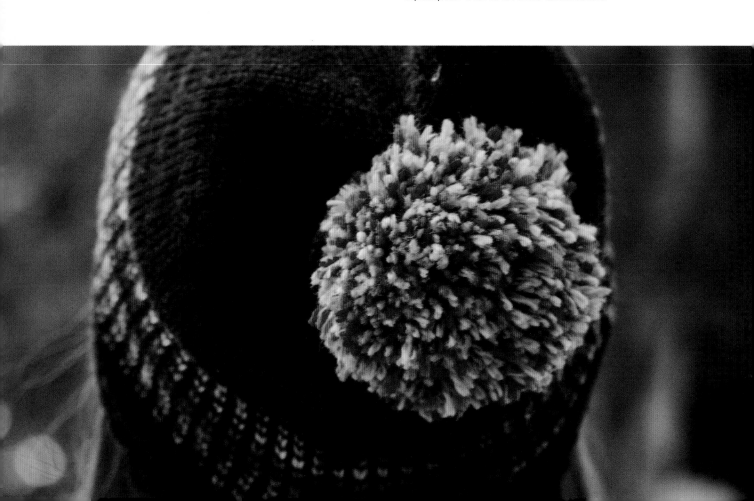

Legend

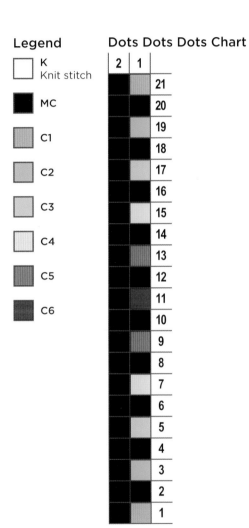

- ☐ **K** Knit stitch
- ■ **MC**
- ▦ **C1**
- ▦ **C2**
- ▦ **C3**
- ▦ **C4**
- ▦ **C5**
- ▦ **C6**

Dots Dots Dots Chart

2	1	
		21
		20
		19
		18
		17
		16
		15
		14
		13
		12
		11
		10
		9
		8
		7
		6
		5
		4
		3
		2
		1

EVORA COWL

by Luise O'Neill

FINISHED MEASUREMENTS
30.5 (60)" circumference x 12.25" high.

YARN
Knit Picks Chroma Fingering
(70% Superwash Wool, 30% Nylon; 396
yards/100g): MC Natural 25248, 1 (2)
ball(s); C1 Lupine 26479, 1 ball.

NEEDLES
US 6 (4mm) 24 (40)" circular needle,
or size to obtain gauge.

US 4 (3.5mm) 24 (40)" circular needle,
or size to obtain gauge.

NOTIONS
Yarn Needle
Stitch Markers

GAUGE
24 sts and 48 rows = 4" over 8-st repeat
of Jacquard Pattern in the rnd with
larger needle, blocked.

20 sts and 40 rows = 4" in Garter st in
the rnd with smaller needle, blocked.

For pattern support, contact
patternsupport@impeccableknits.ca

Notes:
Named for the beautifully eloquent melody "Tango to Evora" by Loreena McKennitt - Canadian composer, singer, pianist, accordionist and harpist - the interlacing jacquard pattern stitch in this cowl is reminiscent of the sway and interplay of her unique music.

This cowl is knit in the round using two colorways – choose two colors that provide good contrast or choose two similar colors for a more subtle design. Carry the unused color up along the inside of the work by twisting it loosely with the current yarn at the end of every other round. The pattern includes stitches that are slipped with the yarn in front; be sure not to pull this yarn tightly but tension the work so that the yarn in front of the slipped stitches lays flat across the work, neither too loose nor too tight. Garter stitch columns divide the front and back jacquard patterns but these can also be worn facing the front or set slightly off-center for a fun twist. There really is no wrong side to this cowl as both the inside and outside of the design have their own beautiful fabric characteristics.

If working from the chart, the chart represents one-half of a round; therefore, each chart row is worked twice. During the first half, stitches inside the red border are repeated to one stitch before the side marker; then, for the second half, the stitches inside the red border are repeated to one stitch before the beginning of rnd marker. The chart is followed from right to left, and read as a RS row.

During blocking, the base and tip of each slipped-stitch pattern rep can be extended to form slightly undulating top and bottom borders.

Jacquard Pattern (worked in the rnd over multiples of 8 sts plus 11)

Using MC:

Rnd 1: K10, *Sl4 WYIF, K4; rep from * to 1 st before M, K1.

Rnd 2: P9, K2, Sl4 WYIF, *K4, Sl4 WYIF; rep from * to 4 sts before M, K4.

Rnd 3: K12, Sl4 WYIF, *K4, Sl4 WYIF; rep from * to 3 sts before M, K3.

Rnd 4: P9, K4, Sl4 WYIF, *K4, Sl4 WYIF; rep from * to 2 sts before M, K2.

Rnd 5: K14, Sl4 WYIF, *K4, Sl4 WYIF; rep from * to 1 st before M, K1.

Rnd 6: P9, K1, Sl1 WYIF, K4, *Sl4 WYIF, K4; rep from * to 4 sts before M, Sl3 WYIF, K1.

Switch to C1:

Rnd 7: K11, Sl4 WYIF, *K4, Sl4 WYIF; rep from * to 4 sts before M, K4.

Rnd 8: P9, K1, *Sl4 WYIF, K4; rep from * to 1 st before M, K1.

Rnd 9: K10, Sl3 WYIF, K4, *Sl4 WYIF, K4; rep from * to 2 sts before M, Sl1 WYIF, K1.

Rnd 10: P9, K1, Sl2 WYIF, K4, *Sl4 WYIF, K4; rep from * to 3 sts before M, Sl2 WYIF K1.

Rnd 11: K10, Sl1 WYIF, K4, *Sl4 WYIF, K4; rep from * to 4 sts before M, Sl3 WYIF, K1.

Rnd 12: P9, K5, Sl4 WYIF, *K4, Sl4 WYIF; rep from * to 1 st before M, K1.

Rep Rnds 1-12 for pattern.

DIRECTIONS

Directions are written for the smaller size; changes for the larger size are given in parentheses. When only one number is given, it applies to both sizes.

Using MC and smaller needle, CO 182 (358) sts. PM to mark beginning of rnd; join in the rnd being careful not to twist the CO sts.

Bottom Border

Work Bottom Border in MC.
Rnd 1: Knit.
Rnd 2: Purl.
Rep last 2 rnds once more, PM after 91 (179) sts in the last rnd. This new M marks the half-way point in the rnd.

Main Pattern

Change to larger needle.

Rnd 1: *Work Jacquard Pattern to M, SM; rep from *.
Rep Rnd 1 until the 12-row Jacquard Pattern has been completed a total of 11.5 times, ending having completed a Rnd 6 of the Jacquard Pattern in MC. 138 rnds of Jacquard Pattern completed. Break C1.

Top Border

Change to smaller needle, work Top Border in MC.
Next Rnd: Knit.
Next Rnd: Purl.
Next Rnd: Knit.
BO sts P-wise.

Finishing

Weave in ends, wash and block to measurements.

Jacquard Pattern Chart

19	18	17	16	15	14	13	12	11	10	9	8	7	6	5	4	3	2	1	
	V	V	V	V						●		●	●	●	●	●	●	●	12
	V	V	V					V											11
	V	V					V	V		●		●	●	●	●	●	●	●	10
	V				V	V	V												9
	V				V	V	V	V		●		●	●	●	●	●	●	●	8
				V	V	V	V												7
	V	V	V					V		●		●	●	●	●	●	●	●	6
	V	V	V	V															5
		V	V	V	V					●		●	●	●	●	●	●	●	4
			V	V	V	V													3
				V	V	V	V			●		●	●	●	●	●	●	●	2
					V	V	V	V											1

Note: Chart is worked twice across the rnd, see Notes.

Legend

☐ **K** Knit stitch	☐ MC	☑V **Slip WYIF** Slip stitch as if to purl with yarn in front.
⬤ **P** Purl stitch	■ C1	☐ Pattern Repeat

FIBONACCI SHAWL

by Rebecca Minner

FINISHED MEASUREMENTS

21" back depth, 88" wide at widest point.

YARN

Knit Picks Stroll Sock Yarn

(75% Fine Superwash Merino Wool, 25% Nylon; 231 yards/50g): MC Black 23701, 4 balls; C1 Blue Topaz 25019, C2 Pucker 26401, C3 Dandelion 25024, C4 Peapod 25026, 1 ball each.

NEEDLES

US 6 (4mm) 24" circular needles, or size to obtain gauge.

NOTIONS

Yarn Needle

GAUGE

23 sts and 45 rows = 4" in Garter stitch, not stretched or blocked (gauge is not critical, any weight of yarn at any gauge can be used but yardage requirements will vary).

Notes:

The shawl's Garter stitch is very stretchy. If you choose to block the finished piece, please be aware that it can, with very little coaxing, grow at least 10" wider than the finished measurements specify.

The size of the shawl is easily adjustable by simply working the Increase Rows to the desired depth of center back (or half of desired width), before beginning the Decrease Rows.

Color changes occur only at the beginning of right side rows. Feel free to change the stripe sequences to suit your needs or tastes; and if stripes aren't your thing, a solid shawl would be equally cozy (with fewer ends to weave in as well).

The Fibonacci Shawl is simply shaped by knitting sideways, from point to point, in Garter stitch with increases and decreases worked along the bottom edge. The semi-random stripes of scrap yarn add interest, but the stripe's adherence to the numbers of the Fibonacci sequence that shows up so often in classical design and proportion helps to keep the chaos in check. Scraps could be picked entirely at random, or colors could be picked specifically for the project, while a solid color provides some continuity throughout the project. Also, thanks to the side-to-side construction, gauge is irrelevant and any weight of yarn can be used: simply knit to the desired depth (or half of desired length) and then begin decreasing for the other half.

Color Sequence
Rows 1-23, 23 rows MC
24-25, 2 rows C1
26-27, 2 rows MC
28-29, 2 rows C1
30-35, 6 rows MC
36-37, 2 rows C4
38-47, 10 rows MC
48-49, 2 rows C2
50-53, 4 rows MC
54-55, 2 rows C3
56-57, 2 rows MC
58-61, Rep Rows 54-57
62-63, 2 rows C3
64-73, 10 rows MC
74-75, 2 rows C4
76-77, 2 rows MC
78-79, 2 rows C4
80-85, 6 rows MC
86-87, 2 rows C2
88-91, 4 rows MC
92-93, 2 rows C1
94-95, 2 rows MC
96-99, Rep Rows 92-95
100-101, 2 rows C1
102-111, 10 rows MC
112-113, 2 rows C3
114-115, 2 rows MC
116-117, 2 rows C3
118-123, 6 rows MC

124-125, 2 rows C1
126-129, 4 rows MC
130-131, 2 rows C4
132-133, 2 rows MC
134-137, Rep Rows 130-133
138-139, 2 rows C4
140-145, 6 rows MC
146-147, 2 rows C2
148-149, 2 rows MC
150-151, 2 rows C2
152-155, 4 rows MC
156-157, 2 rows C3
158-167, 10 rows MC
168-169, 2 rows C4
170-171, 2 rows MC
172-173, 2 rows C4
174-183, 10 rows MC
184-185, 2 rows C3
186-189, 4 rows MC
190-191, 2 rows C1
192-193, 2 rows MC
194-195, 2 rows C1
196-199, 4 rows MC
200-201, 2 rows C2
202-203, 2 rows MC
204-207, Rep Rows 200-203
208-209, 2 rows C2
210-215, 6 rows MC
216-217, 2 rows C3
218-227, 10 rows MC
228-229, 2 rows C4
230-233, 4 rows MC
234-235, 2 rows C1
236-237, 2 rows MC
238-241, Rep Rows 234-237
242-243, 2 rows C1
244-249, 6 rows MC
250-251, 2 rows C2
252-253, 2 rows MC
254-255, 2 rows C2
256-265, 10 rows MC
266-267, 2 rows C1
268-269, 2 rows MC
270-271, 2 rows C1
272-275, 4 rows MC
276-277, 2 rows C4
278-279, 2 rows MC
280-283, Rep Rows 276-279
284-285, 2 rows C4
286-291, 6 rows MC
292-293, 2 rows C2
294-295, 2 rows MC
296-297, 2 rows C2
298-301, 4 rows MC
302-303, 2 rows C3
304-307, 4 rows MC
308-309, 2 rows C1

310-319, 10 rows MC
320-321, 2 rows C2
322-327, 6 rows MC
328-329, 2 rows C3
330-331, 2 rows MC
332-335, Rep Rows 328-331
336-337, 2 rows C3
338-343, 6 rows MC
344-345, 2 rows C4
346-347, 2 rows MC
348-349, 2 rows C4
350-359, 10 rows MC
360-361, 2 rows C1
362-363, 2 rows MC
364-365, 2 rows C1
366-369, 4 rows MC
370-371, 2 rows C3
372-377, 6 rows MC
378-379, 2 rows C4
380-383, 4 rows MC
384-385, 2 rows C2
386-387, 2 rows MC
388-391, Rep Rows 384-387
392-393, 2 rows C2
394-399, 6 rows MC
400-401, 2 rows C3
402-403, 2 rows MC
404-405, 2 rows C3
406-415, 10 rows MC
416-417, 2 rows C2
418-423, 6 rows MC
424-425, 2 rows C1
426-427, 2 rows MC
428-431, Rep Rows 424-427
432-433, 2 rows C1
434-437, 4 rows MC
438-439, 2 rows C4
440-441, 2 rows MC
442-443, 2 rows C4
444-449, 6 rows MC
450-451, 2 rows C2
452-455, 4 rows MC
456-457, 2 rows C3
458-459, 2 rows MC
460-461, 2 rows C3
462-471, 10 rows MC
472-473, 2 rows C4
474-475 2 rows MC
476-479, Rep Rows 472-475
480-481, 2 rows C4
482-487, 6 rows MC
488-489, 2 rows C1
490-493, 4 rows MC
494-495, 2 rows C3
496-499, 4 rows MC
500-501, 2 rows C1
502-503, 2 rows MC

504-505, 2 rows C1
506-515, 10 rows MC
516-517, 2 rows C4
518-519, 2 rows MC
520-521, 2 rows C4
522-527, 6 rows MC
528-529, 2 rows C2
530-531, 2 rows MC
532-535, Rep Rows 528-531
536-537, 2 rows C2
538-541, 4 rows MC
542-543, 2 rows C3
544-549, 6 rows MC
550-551, 2 rows C1
552-553, 2 rows MC
554-555, 2 rows C1
556-559, 4 rows MC
560-561, 2 rows C2
562-571, 10 rows MC
572-573, 2 rows C4
574-577, 4 rows MC
578-579, 2 rows C3
580-581, 2 rows MC
582-585, Rep Rows 578-581
586-587, 2 rows C3
588-597, 10 rows MC
598-599, 2 rows C1
600-603, 4 rows MC
604-605, 2 rows C4
606-607, 2 rows MC
608-609, 2 rows C4
610-615, 6 rows MC
616-617, 2 rows C2
618-623, 6 rows MC
624-625, 2 rows C1
626-627, 2 rows MC
628-629, 2 rows C1
630-633, 4 rows MC
634-635, 2 rows C4
636-637, 2 rows MC
638-641, Rep Rows 634-637
642-643, 2 rows C4
644-647, 4 rows MC
648-649, 2 rows C3
650-659, 10 rows MC
660-661, 2 rows C2
662-663, 2 rows MC
664-665, 2 rows C2
666-671, 6 rows MC
672-673, 2 rows C1
674-677, 4 rows MC
678-679, 2 rows C4
680-683, 4 rows MC
684-685, 2 rows C3
686-687, 2 rows MC

688-689, 2 rows C3
690-693, 4 rows MC
694-695, 2 rows C2
696-705, 10 rows MC
706-707, 2 rows C3
708-711, 4 rows MC
712-713, 2 rows C1
714-715, 2 rows MC
716-719, Rep Rows 712-715
720-721, 2 rows C1
722-727, 6 rows MC
728-729, 2 rows C4
730-731, 2 rows MC
732-733, 2 rows C4
734-739, 6 rows MC
740-741, 2 rows C2
742-751, 10 rows MC
752-753, 2 rows C2
754-757, 4 rows MC
758-759, 2 rows C4
760-765, 6 rows MC
766-767, 2 rows C3
768-771, 4 rows MC,
772-773, 2 rows C1
774-775, 2 rows MC
776-777, 2 rows C1
778-783, 6 rows MC
784-785, 2 rows C3
786-787, 2 rows MC
788-791, Rep Rows 784-787
792-793, 2 rows C3
794-797, 4 rows MC
798-799, 2 rows C1
800-809, 10 rows MC
810-811, 2 rows C4
812-813, 2 rows MC
814-815, 2 rows C4
816-819, 4 rows MC
820-821, 2 rows C2
822-827, 6 rows MC
828-829, 2 rows C3
830-835, 6 rows MC
836-837, 2 rows C1
838-839, 2 rows MC
840-841, 2 rows C1
842-851, 10 rows MC
852-853, 2 rows C2
854-855, 2 rows MC
856-859, Rep Rows 852-855
860-861, 2 rows C2
862-867, 6 rows MC
868-869, 2 rows C4
870-879, 10 rows MC
880-881, 2 rows C1
882-883, 2 rows MC

884-885, 2 rows C1
886-889, 4 rows MC
890-891, 2 rows C4
892-897, 6 rows MC
898-899, 2 rows C3
900-901, 2 rows MC
902-903, 2 rows C3
904-913, 10 rows MC
914-915, 2 rows C2
916-919, 4 rows MC
920-921, 2 rows C1
922-923, 2 rows MC
924-927, Rep Rows 920-923
928-929, 2 rows C1
930-935, 6 rows MC
936-937, 2 rows C4
938-939, 2 rows MC
940-941, 2 rows C4
942-945, 4 rows MC
946-947, 2 rows C3
948-953, 6 rows MC
954-955, 2 rows C2
956-957, 2 rows MC
958-959, 2 rows C2
960-983, 24 rows MC

DIRECTIONS

Using MC, CO 2 sts.

Set Up
Begin working the Color Sequence, above, starting with Row 1.

Row 1 (WS): K.

Row 2 (RS): K1, YO, K1. 3 sts.

Row 3: K1, K1 TBL, K1.

Rows 4 and 5: K.

Increase Rows
Row 6 (RS): K2, YO, K to end. 1 st inc.

Row 7 (WS): K to YO, K1 TBL, K2.

Rows 8 and 9: K.

Rep Increase Rows 6-9 while continuing to work the Color Sequence, until 493 rows have been worked from CO. 125 sts.

Decrease Rows
Row 494: K1, SSK, K to end. 1 st dec.

Rows 495-497: K.

Rep Decrease Rows 494-497 while continuing to work the Color Sequence as established until 981 rows have been worked from CO. 3 sts.

Row 982: K1, SSK. 2 sts.

Row 983: K.

BO remaining 2 sts.

Finishing
Weave in ends.

FIREBRICKS COWL

by Mone Dräger

FINISHED MEASUREMENTS

24" circumference x 8" high.

YARN

Knit Picks Swish Worsted
(100% Superwash Merino Wool; 110 yards/50g): MC White 24662, C1 Hollyberry 25148, C2 Allspice 24297, C3 Copper 23882, C4 Honey 26066, 1 ball each.

NEEDLES

US 6 (4mm) 16" circular needle, or size to obtain gauge.

NOTIONS

Stitch Marker
Cable Needle
Yarn Needle

GAUGE

20 sts and 40 rows = 4" over Bricks pattern in the rnd, blocked.

For pattern support, contact
mone.draeger@gmx.de

Notes:

The differently colored garter stitch stripes on the neutral background get sectioned by the slipped stitches and seem to form bricks – just like bricks in a country-style brick wall.

The cowl is knit in the round. The number of stitches cast on sets the circumference of the cowl. To work a tighter or wider cowl, adjust the stitch count with a multiple of 8 sts and work fewer or more repeats of the Bricks pattern.

The cowl could be worked using only two colors for a more subdued look, or as many colors as there are stripes. Choose your favorite colors to make your Bricks cowl unique!

The chart refers to MC and CC only. Use the provided color sequence for the stripes or pick your own colors for each stripe worked in CC.

Except for the MC, the yarn is not carried along unless only one CC is used. Each CC strand gets broken when a CC stripe has been finished. To avoid having to weave in multiple yarns when the shawl is completed, weave in the ends while knitting.

When following the chart, read each row from right to left as a RS row.

Bricks Pattern (worked in the rnd over a multiple of 8 sts)
Rnd 1: In MC, K1, (K1 with DW) twice, K5.
Rnd 2: In CC, K1, (Sl1 WYIB dropping second wrap) twice, K5.
Rnd 3: In CC, P1, Sl2 WYIB, P5.
Rnd 4: In CC, K1, Sl2 WYIB, K5.
Rnd 5: Rep Rnd 3.
Rnd 6: In MC, RT, LT, K4.
Rnd 7: In MC, K5, (K1 with DW) twice, K1.
Rnd 8: In CC, K5, (Sl1 WYIB dropping second wrap) twice, K1.
Rnd 9: In CC, P5, Sl2 WYIB, P1.
Rnd 10: In CC, K5, Sl2 WYIB, K1.
Rnd 11: Rep Rnd 9.
Rnd 12: In MC, K4, RT, LT.
Rep Rnds 1-12 for pattern.

Color Sequence
Garter Stripe 1: C1
Garter Stripe 2: C2
Garter Stripe 3: C3
Garter Stripe 4: C4
Garter Stripe 5: C2
Garter Stripe 6: C1
Garter Stripe 7: C4
Garter Stripe 8: C3
Garter Stripe 9: C1
Garter Stripe 10: C2
Garter Stripe 11: C3
Garter Stripe 12: C4

Double Wrap (DW)
To avoid negative ease caused by the slipped sts used in the cables, they are worked with double wraps. When the st is knit, the yarn is wrapped twice around the needle; the additional wrap is dropped when working the st the next time.

Left Twist (LT): Sl next st to CN and place at front of work, K1, then K1 from CN.
Right Twist (RT): Skip the 1st st, knit into the 2nd st, then knit skipped st. Slip both sts off LH needle.

Weave in yarn ends while knitting: Introduce the new color approximately 10-12 sts before it is needed. Hold the tail to the right, the working yarn with your needle to the left. Insert the RH needle into the next st, duck under the 'new' yarn to catch the 'old' yarn and pull it through. For the next st, insert the RH needle into the st, but catch the 'old' yarn over the 'new yarn' and pull it through. Rep these steps to the point where the 'new' yarn is needed. When the color is no longer needed, rep the same steps, knitting with the 'new' yarn and carrying the 'old' yarn along to be woven in.

DIRECTIONS

Bottom Edge
In MC, loosely CO 120 sts. Join to work in the rnd and PM, being careful not to twist sts.
Rnd 1: P.
Rnd 2: K.
Rep Rnds 1-2 once more.

Body
Work Bricks pattern 15 times across the rnd. Work Rnds 1-12 of Bricks pattern a total of 6 times, and join and use CCs as per the provided color sequence or choose as desired. Break CC after each completed garter stripe unless only one CC is used.

Top Edge
Worked in MC.
Rnd 1: K.
Rnd 2: P.
Rep Rnds 1-2 once more. BO loosely.

Finishing
Weave in ends, wash and block.

Bricks Chart

8	7	6	5	4	3	2	1	
RT	LT	RT	LT					12
•	V	V	•	•	•	•	•	11
	V	V						10
•	V	V	•	•	•	•	•	9
	▽	▽						8
	②	②						7
				RT	LT	RT	LT	6
•	•	•	•	•	V	V	•	5
					V	V		4
•	•	•	•	•	V	V	•	3
					▽	▽		2
					②	②		1

Legend

☐ **K**
Knit stitch

● **P**
Purl stitch

▽ **Sl1 WYIB Dropping Second Wrap**

② **Double Wrap (DW)**
When the st is knit, the yarn is wrapped twice around the needle; the additional wrap is dropped when working the st the next time.

⧅ **Left Twist (LT)**
Sl1 to CN, hold in front. K1, K1 from CN.

⧄ **Right Twist (RT)**
Skip the 1st st, knit into 2nd st, then knit skipped st. Slip both sts off LH needle.

■ **MC**

☐ **CC**

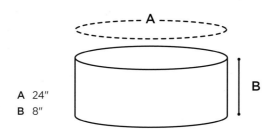

A 24"
B 8"

FROSTED MITTENS

by Emily Kintigh

FINISHED MEASUREMENTS

7 (7.5, 8)" hand circumference x 10.5 (11.75, 12.75)" mitten length or 7 (7.75, 8)" fingerless mitt length.

YARN

Knit Picks Alux

(66% Baby Alpaca, 34% Lurex; 181 yards/50g): C1 Sapphire 27566, C2 Sky 27563, C3 Whirlpool 27562, C4 Pennyroyal 27564; 1 ball each.

NEEDLES

US 2 (3mm) DPNs or two 24" circular needles for two circulars technique, or one 32" or longer circular needle for Magic Loop technique, or one size below gauge needle.

US 3 (3.25mm) DPNs or two 24" circular needles for two circulars technique, or one 32" or longer circular needle for Magic Loop technique, or size to obtain gauge.

NOTIONS

Yarn Needle
Stitch Markers
Scrap Yarn or Stitch Holder

GAUGE

32 sts and 32 rnds = 4" over Frosted Chart in the round, blocked.

Notes:

The mittens are worked in the round from the cuff up. Stitches are held to be worked later for the thumb. The pattern also includes instructions for a fingerless mitt version.

The charts are worked in the rnd; read each row from right to left as a RS row.

M1L (Make 1 Left-leaning stitch): PU the bar between st just worked and next st and place on LH needle as a regular stitch; K TBL.

M1R (Make 1 Right-leaning stitch): PU the bar between st just worked and next st and place on LH needle backwards (incorrect stitch mount). K TFL.

2x2 Ribbing (in the rnd over a multiple of 4 sts)
All Rnds: (K2, P2) to end.

1x1 Ribbing (in the rnd over a multiple of 2 sts)
All Rnds: (K1, P1) to end.

DIRECTIONS

Mittens
Cuff
With smaller needles and C1, loosely CO 56 (60, 64) sts. PM and join in the rnd being careful not to twist the sts. Work in 2x2 Ribbing until cuff measures 2.75 (3, 3.25)" from CO edge.

Main Mitten
Switch to larger needles. With C2, K 1 rnd.
Work Rnd 1 of the Thumb Gusset Chart; rep Sts 1-2 to the end of the rnd, PM for thumb gusset, work chart the rest of the rnd. 1 gusset st made between markers on Rnd 1. Cont working from Thumb Gusset Chart; rep Sts 1-2 to the thumb gusset M, work the rest of the chart between the gusset M and the end of the rnd M. Work through Rnd 22 (24, 26).

Work Rnd 1 (3, 5) of Frosted Chart to gusset M, remove M and place the 21 (23, 25) thumb sts on scrap yarn or st holder. Cont working in the rnd from Frosted Chart.

For Mittens
7" Size: Work Rnds 2-21, then Rnds 1-9. Using C2 only, move on to Rnd 3 of Decreases.
7.5" Size: Work Rnds 4-21, then Rnds 1-13. Cont working with C3 only, (K13, K2tog) to end. 56 sts. Move on to Rnd 2 of Decreases.
8" Size: Work Rnds 6-21, then Rnds 1-17. Using C4 only, move on to Rnd 1 of Decreases.

For Fingerless Mitts
7" Size: Work Rnds 2-6. Move on to Fingerless Mitt Cuff.
7.5" Size: Work Rnds 4-10. Move on to Fingerless Mitt Cuff.
8" Size: Work Rnds 6-14. Move on to Fingerless Mitt Cuff.

Fingerless Mitt Cuff

Switch to smaller needles and C1. Work in 2x2 Ribbing for .75". Loosely BO all sts. Move on to Thumb.

Decreases

Rnd 1: (K6, K2tog) to end. 56 sts.
Rnd 2: K to end.
Rnd 3: (K5, K2tog) to end. 48 sts.
Rnd 4: K to end.
Rnd 5: (K4, K2tog) to end. 40 sts.
Rnd 6: K to end.
Rnd 7: (K3, K2tog) to end. 32 sts.
Rnd 8: K to end.
Rnd 9: (K2, K2tog) to end. 24 sts.
Rnd 10: K to end.
Rnd 11: (K1, K2tog) to end. 16 sts.
Rnd 12: K2tog to end. 8 sts.
Cut yarn and pull through remaining sts. Move on to Thumb.

Thumb (Mittens and Fingerless Mitts)

Place 21 (23, 25) sts held for thumb on larger needles. PM and begin working in the rnd.
Rnd 1: With C2 (C3, C1) K2tog, then work Rnd 1 (3, 5) of Frosted Chart, starting with the second st, to end. Cont working from Frosted Chart. 20 (22, 24) sts.

For Mittens

7" Size: Work Rnds 2-13. Cont working with C3 only, (K8, K2tog) to end. 18 sts. Move on to Rnd 2 of Thumb Decreases.
7.5" Size: Work Rnds 4-17. Cont working with C4 only, (K4, K2tog, K3, K2tog) to end. 18 sts. Move on to Rnd 2 of Thumb Decreases.
8" Size: Work Rnds 6-21. Using C2 only, move on to Rnd 1 of Thumb Decreases.

For Fingerless Mitts

7" Size: Work chart Rnds 2-3.
7.5" Size: Work chart Rnds 4-6.
8" Size: Work chart Rnds 6-10.

All Sizes: Switch to smaller needles and C1. Work in 1x1 Ribbing for .75". Loosely BO all sts.

Thumb Decreases

Rnd 1: (K2, K2tog) to end. 18 sts.
Rnd 2: K to end.
Rnd 3: (K1, K2tog) to end. 12 sts.
Rnd 4: K2tog to end. 6 sts.
Cut yarn and pull through remaining sts.

Finishing

Weave in ends, making sure to close up the hole where the thumb meets the hand. Wash and block to measurements.

Legend

K
Knit stitch

M **Make One Left**
Pick up the bar between stitch just worked and the next stitch on needle, inserting LH needle from front to back; purl through the backloop.

MR **Make One Right**
Pick up the bar between stitch just worked and the next stitch on needle, inserting LH needle from back to front; knit through the front loop.

Pattern Repeat

No Stitch

C1

C2

C3

C4

Frosted Chart

2	1	
		21
		20
	C1	19
C1		18
C4		17
	C1	16
C1	C3	15
C3		14
		13
	C1	12
C1		11
		10
	C1	9
C1	C4	8
C4		7
	C1	6
	C1	5
C1	C3	4
C3		3
	C1	2
C1	C2	1

Thumb Gusset Chart

INTENSIFY SHAWL

by Mone Dräger

FINISHED MEASUREMENTS
68" wide along top edge, 29" high.

YARN

Knit Picks Palette
(100% Peruvian Highland Wool; 231
yards/50g): MC Celadon 24254, 2 balls;
C1 Hare Heather 26042, C2 Edamame
24257, C3 Clover 24256, C4 Forest
Heather 24584, C5 Aurora Heather
25537, 1 ball each.

NEEDLES
US 2 (3mm) 40" circular needle, or size
to obtain gauge.

NOTIONS
Stitch Markers
Yarn Needle

GAUGE
26 sts and 32 rows = 4" over Stockinette
stitch, blocked.
Gauge is not crucial for the project, but
will influence the size of the finished
shawl and amount of yarn required.

Notes:

The shawl is knit from the top down. Small garter stitch stripes using five contrast colors alternate with stockinette parts in a neutral background color. The contrast colors are used in the same color sequence in each section but the stockinette stripes become smaller with each repeat worked, so that the colorful garter stitch stripes become more prominent with each section worked.

Except for the MC (unless otherwise stated), the yarn is not carried along, but gets broken after each stripe worked. To avoid having to weave in multiple yarns when the shawl is finished, weave in the ends while knitting.

The final garter border in contrast colors is worked in two parts: one half in horizontal stripes as established, the second half in vertical garter stripes worked sideways. Alternatively, the complete border can be worked in horizontal stripes if desired, working increases as established in the pattern.

Weave in yarn ends while knitting: When the new yarn is needed in a WS row: Introduce the new color approximately 12 sts before it is needed. Hold the tail to the right, the working yarn with your needle to the left. Insert the RH needle into the next st, duck under the 'new' yarn to catch the 'old' yarn and pull it through. For the next st, insert the RH needle into the st, but catch the 'old' yarn over the 'new yarn' and pull it through. Rep these steps to the point where the 'new' yarn is needed. When the color is no longer needed, rep the same steps, knitting with the 'new' yarn and carrying the 'old' yarn along to be woven in.
When the new yarn is needed in a RS row: Work as above until you reach the last 3 sts, then SL1 WYIF, SL next st and work a YO with the new yarn at the same time (bring the yarn from the front over the needle to the back and between the needles to the front again), SL last st. On the next row, K the YO together with the st.

M1PL: Using the LH needle, pick up the bar of yarn between the needles from the front, then P the newly picked up st TBL.

M1PR: Using the LH needle, pick up the bar of yarn between the needles from the back, then P the newly picked up st.

Double Stitch (DS)
Bring the working yarn in front, slip the next st P-wise, bring the working yarn from front to back over the needle and pull on it enough to bring the legs of that st over the needle. The st on the needle looks like a double st. When working the DS the next time, K into both legs and treat as one st.

DIRECTIONS

Body
Set-up
With MC, CO 3 sts.
Knit 14 rows. At the end of the last row, do not turn, but rotate the piece 90 degrees clockwise. PU and K 7 sts along the top edge; 1 st into each of the garter ridges. Rotate the piece 90 degrees clockwise again. PU and K 3 sts from the CO edge. 13 sts.
Row 1 (WS): K3, PM, M1PL, P4, PM, P3, M1PR, PM, K3. 15 sts.
Row 2 (RS): K3, SM, M1L, K to M, M1R, SM, K1, M1L, K to M, M1R, SM, K3. 4 sts inc, 19 sts.
Row 3: K3, SM, M1PL, P to last 3 sts, M1PR, SM, K3. 2 sts inc, 21 sts.
Rep Rows 2 – 3 nine more times. 75 sts. Join C1 on last row.

Segment 1
Row 1 (RS): With C1, K3, SM, M1L, K to M, M1R, SM, K1, M1L, K to M, M1R, SM, K3. 4 sts inc, 79 sts.
Row 2 (WS): With C1, K3, SM, M1L, K to last 3 sts, M1R, SM, K3. 2 sts inc, 81 sts.
Row 3: With MC, K3, SM, M1L, K to M, M1R, SM, K1, M1L, K to M, M1R, SM, K3. 4 sts inc, 85 sts.
Row 4: With MC, K3, SM, M1PL, P to last 3 sts, M1PR, SM, K3. 2 sts inc, 87 sts.
Rows 5-6: Rep Rows 3-4. 93 sts.
Rep Rows 1-6 four more times, using C2, C3, C4 and C5 instead of C1. 165 sts. Rep Rows 3-4 five more times. 195 sts.

Segment 2
Row 1 (RS): With C1, K3, SM, M1L, K to M, M1R, SM, K1, M1L, K to M, M1R, SM, K3. 4 sts inc, 199 sts.
Row 2 (WS): With C1, K3, SM, M1L, K to last 3 sts, M1R, SM, K3. 2 sts inc, 201 sts.
Row 3: With MC, K3, SM, M1L, K to M, M1R, SM, K1, M1L, K to M, M1R, SM, K3. 4 sts inc, 205 sts.

Row 4: With MC, K3, SM, M1PL, P to last 3 sts, M1PR, SM, K3. 2 sts inc, 207 sts.
Row 5: Rep Row 3. 211 sts.
Row 6: With C2, K3, SM, M1PL, P to last 3 sts, M1PR, SM, K3. 2 sts inc, 213 sts.
Row 7: With C2, K3, SM, M1PL, P to M, M1PR, SM, P1, M1PL, P to M, M1PL, SM, K3. 4 sts inc, 217 sts.
Row 8: With MC, K3, SM, M1PL, P to last 3 sts, M1PR, SM, K3. 2 sts inc, 219 sts.
Row 9: Rep Row 3. 223 sts.
Row 10: Rep Row 4. 225 sts.
Rep Rows 1-10 once more, using C3 and C4 instead of C1 and C2. Then rep Rows 1-2 once more, using C5 instead of C1. 261 sts.
Next Row: With MC, K3, SM, M1L, K to M, M1R, SM, K1, M1L, K to M, M1R, SM, K3. 4 sts inc, 265 sts.
Next Row: With MC, K3, SM, M1PL, P to last 3 sts, M1PR, SM, K3. 2 sts inc, 267 sts.
Rep last 2 rows five more times. 297 sts.

Segment 3
Row 1 (RS): With C1, K3, SM, M1L, K to M, M1R, SM, K1, M1L, K to M, M1R, SM, K3. 4 sts inc, 301 sts.
Row 2 (WS): With C1, K3, SM, M1L, K to last 3 sts, M1R, SM, K3. 2 sts inc, 303 sts.
Row 3: With MC, K3, SM, M1L, K to M, M1R, SM, K1, M1L, K to M, M1R, SM, K3. 4 sts inc, 307 sts.
Row 4: With MC, K3, SM, M1PL, P to last 3 sts, M1PR, SM, K3. 2 sts inc, 309 sts.
Rep Rows 1-4 four more times, using C2, C3, C4 and C5 instead of C1. 357 sts.
Rep Rows 3-4 four more times. 381 sts.

Segment 4
Row 1 (RS): With C1, K3, SM, M1L, K to M, M1R, SM, K1, M1L, K to M, M1R, SM, K3. 4 sts inc, 385 sts.
Row 2 (WS): With C1, K3, SM, M1L, K to last 3 sts, M1R, SM, K3. 2 sts inc, 387 sts.
Row 3: With MC, K3, SM, M1L, K to M, M1R, SM, K1, M1L, K to M, M1R, SM, K3. 4 sts inc, 391 sts.
Row 4: With C2, K3, SM, M1PL, P to last 3 sts, M1PR, SM, K3. 2 sts inc, 393 sts.
Row 5: With C2, K3, SM, M1PL, P to M, M1PR, SM, P1, M1PL, P to M, M1PL, SM, K3. 4 sts inc, 397 sts.
Row 6: With MC, K3, SM, M1PL, P to last 3 sts, M1PR, SM, K3. 2 sts inc, 399 sts.
Rep Rows 1-6 once more, using C3 and C4 instead of C1 and C2. Then rep Rows 1-2 once more, using C5 instead of C1. 423 sts.
Next Row: With MC, K3, SM, M1L, K to M, M1R, SM, K1, M1L, K to M, M1R, SM, K3. 4 sts inc, 427 sts.
Next Row: With MC, K3, SM, M1PL, P to last 3 sts, M1PR, SM, K3. 2 sts inc, 429 sts.
Rep last 2 rows three more times. 447 sts. Break MC.

Segment 5

Row 1 (RS): With C1, K3, SM, M1L, K to M, M1R, SM, K1, M1L, K to M, M1R, SM, K3. 4 sts inc, 451 sts.

Row 2 (WS): With C1, K3, SM, M1L, K to last 3 sts, M1R, SM, K3. 2 sts inc, 453 sts.

Rep Rows 1-2 four more times, using C2, C3, C4 and C5 instead of C1. 477 sts. Join MC.

Next Row: With MC, K3, SM, M1L, K to M, M1R, SM, K1, M1L, K to M, M1R, SM, K3. 4 sts inc, 481 sts.

Next Row: With MC, K3, SM, M1PL, P to last 3 sts, M1PR, SM, K3. 483 sts.

Rep last 2 rows two more times. 2 sts inc, 495 sts. Break MC.

Right Border

The right border (as worked, it will be the LH side when worn) will be worked over the first 248 sts; keep remaining 247 sts on hold for left border.

Row 1 (RS): With C1, K3, SM, M1L, K to M, M1R, SM, K1. 2 sts inc, 250 sts.

Row 2 (WS): With C1, K to last 3 sts, M1R, SM, K3. 1 st inc, 251 sts.

Row 3-4: Rep Rows 1-2. 254 sts.

Rep Rows 1-4 four times using C2, C3, C4 and then C5 instead of C1. 278 sts.

BO sts as follows: K1, *K1, return both sts to LH needle, K2tog TBL; rep from * until all sts of right border are bound off, keep remaining loop on RH needle.

Left Border

With RS facing and starting next to the remaining st from BO, using C5, PU and K10 from the edge of the right border; 1 st from each garter ridge. 11 sts on RH needle, 247 sts on LH needle. The set-up segment is worked over the first 11 sts only. Turn work.

Set-up Segment

Short-Row 1 (WS): K10, Sl1 WYIF, turn.

Short-Row 2 (RS): K1 TBL, K1, turn.

Short-Row 3: DS, Sl1 WYIF, turn.

Short-Row 4: K1 TBL, K to 1 st past DS created in previous row, turn.

Short-Row 5: DS, K to last st, Sl1 WYIF, turn.

Rep Short-Rows 4-5 eight more times.

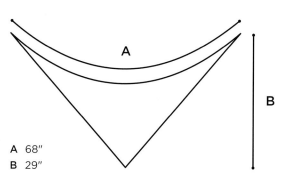

A 68"
B 29"

Main Segment

On each RS row worked, the last st of the border is worked together with the first st of the shawl's body. Begin with C5.

Row 1 (RS): K1 TBL, K9, SSK with next live body st, turn.

Row 2 (WS): K10, Sl1 WYIF, turn.

Rep Rows 1-2 nine more times. 11 sts on RH needle, 237 sts on LH needle.

With C4, C3, C2, then C1, work Rows 1-2 ten times each. 11 sts on RH needle, 197 sts on LH needle.

Keeping the color sequence C5, C4, C3, C2, C1, work Rows 1-2 nine times each, then 8 times each, then 7 times each, then 6 times each, then 5 times each. 11 sts on RH needle, 22 sts on LH needle.

With C5, C4, C3, C2, C1 work Rows 1-2 four times each. 11 st on RH needle, 2 sts on LH needle.

Final Segment

Short-Row 1 (RS): K1 TBL, K10, turn.

Short-Row 2 (WS): DS, K to last st, Sl1 WYIF, turn.

Short-Row 3: K1 TBL, K to 1 st before DS created in previous row, turn.

Short-Row 4: DS, K to last st, Sl1 WYIF, turn.

Rep Short-Rows 3-4 eight more times.

Next Row: K1 TBL, K9, SSK, turn. 11 sts on RH needle, 1 st on LH needle.

Next Row: K10, M1L, Sl1 WYIF, turn. 12 sts on RH needle, 1 st on LH needle.

Next Row: K1 TBL, K10, SSK, turn. 12 sts.

Next Row: K12, turn.

BO as follows: K1, *K1, return both sts to LH needle, K2tog TBL; rep from * to end. Draw yarn through remaining st and fasten off.

Finishing

Weave in ends, wash and block.

JASMINE SLIPPERS

by Meredith Wills

FINISHED MEASUREMENTS

8.75 (9.25, 9.75)" finished slipper length; to correspond to US Women's shoe size 7 (8, 9); slipper is meant to be worn snugly.

YARN

Knit Picks Hawthorne Multi

(80% Superwash Fine Highland Wool, 20% Polymide; 357 yards/100g): Cully 27416; 1 skein, or approximately 285 yards.

NEEDLES

US 0 (2mm) straight or circular needles, or size to obtain gauge.

US 1.5 (2.5mm) or smaller; two 24" circular needles or one 40" or longer circular needle, for picking up Instep edge sts (optional).

US 3 (3.5mm) two 24" circular needles for two circulars technique, or one 40" or longer circular needle for Magic Loop technique, or size to obtain gauge.

NOTIONS

Scrap Yarn, fingering weight
Small Cable Needle
Stitch Marker
Yarn Needle, large eyed
Sewing Needle, Thread, and Pins
Elastic Cord

GAUGE

50 sts and 54 rows = 4" in Main Cable pattern on smaller needles, blocked.

24 sts and 36 rows = 4" in St st in the rnd with yarn held double on larger needles, blocked.

Notes:

Stashbusting is not mutually exclusive from elegance. With their feminine shape and delicate Bavarian-stitch cabling, these Jasmine Slippers will make you feel like a princess.

Unlike most footwear, the instep is worked as a cabled strip with rolled edges and a tapered end. The bottom edge of the strip is then overlapped by the tapered end and joined, after which the surprisingly durable sole is worked in the round using two strands of yarn. Short rows shape the foot, and elastic threaded along the instep edge guarantees a snug fit.

When working the charts, read RS rows (even numbers) from right to left, and WS rows (odd numbers) from left to right. All charts begin on a WS row.

Wrap and Turn (W&T)

Work until the st to be wrapped. If knitting: bring yarn to the front of the work, slip next st as if to purl, return the yarn to the back; turn work and slip wrapped st onto RH needle. Continue across row. If purling: bring yarn to the back of the work, slip next st as if to purl, return the yarn to the front; turn work and slip wrapped st onto RH needle. Continue across row. Picking up wraps: Work to the wrapped st. If knitting, insert the RH needle under the wrap(s), then through the wrapped st K-wise. Knit the wrap(s) together with the wrapped st. If purling, slip the wrapped st P-wise onto the RH needle, and use the LH needle to lift the wrap(s) and place them on the RH needle. Slip wrap(s) and unworked st back to LH needle; purl all tog TBL.

Kitchener Stitch: Follow the instructions provided on the Knit Picks website here:
http://tutorials.knitpicks.com/wptutorials/kitchener-stitch/

5-St Decrease: Sl 3 sts to RH needle. *On RH needle, pass 2nd st from needle tip over first and off needle. Sl remaining st back to LH needle. On LH needle, pass 2nd st from needle over 1st st and off needle.* Sl remaining st back to RH needle. Rep from * to *. 4 sts dec.

DIRECTIONS

Right Slipper

Instep

The instep is worked flat, so some cables will be done on WS rows.

Using scrap yarn, CO 21 sts on largest needle.

Instep Setup Rows

Row 1 (WS): Using largest needle and working yarn, P21.

Row 2 (RS): Switch to smallest needles. K2, P17, K2.

Row 3: Sl1, P1, K17, P2.

Row 4: Sl2, P17, K2.

With RS facing, instep will have two Sl sts on the right side and one Sl st on the left.

Main Cable

Next Row (WS): Sl1, P1, work Row 1 of Main Cable Chart for your size, P2.

Next Row (RS): Sl2, work Row 2 of Main Cable Chart for your size, K2.

Cont as established, working Main Cable Chart for your size through Row 23 (3, 15), then rep Rows 24-55 (4-35, 16-47) 5 (6, 6) times. Work Rows 24-50 (4-30, 16-42) once.

Toe Cable

Next **Row (WS):** Sl1, P1, work Row 1 of Toe Cable Chart, P2.

Next Row (RS): Sl2, work Row 2 of Toe Cable Chart, K2.

Cont as established, working through Toe Cable Chart once, ending with a WS row.

Toe Finishing

Row 1 (RS): Sl2, P1, K2.

Row 2 (WS): Work 5-st Decrease.

Cut a 20" tail. BO by threading tail through remaining st. Block cabled section of Instep to measurements, inside the Sl st edges.

Sole

Read through entire section carefully before beginning. Remove scrap yarn from CO edge and place sts on smallest needle. Use circular needles to PU but NOT knit one st for each slipped st along left edge of instep (the edge with only one slipped st). 61 (64, 67) sts on each needle, 122 (128, 134) sts total. Join slipped sts in the rnd, moving 4 sts from RH needle to LH needle. PM to mark beginning of rnd.

Using largest circular needles and two strands of yarn held together, work Sole Setup Rnd.

Sole Setup Rnd: K4. Place CO edge beneath slipped sts at toe, with RS of CO edge facing up. (Both ends should have the RS facing up, with the tapered end overlapping the CO end. This will form a "teardrop" shape.) For next 20 sts, work in CO edge by knitting each slipped st tog with a CO st TBL. K to end of rnd.

Next Rnd: K.

Toe Decrease/Short Rows

Row 1 (RS): K13 (13, 14), K2tog, K15 (16, 16), W&T. 1 st dec.
Row 2 (WS): P42 (43, 45), Ssp, P15 (16, 16), W&T. 1 st dec.
Row 3: K41 (42, 44), K2tog, K12 (13, 13), W&T. 1 st dec.
Row 4: P37 (38, 40), Ssp, P12 (13, 13), W&T. 1 st dec.
Row 5: K27 (28, 29), K2tog, K2, K2tog, K3 (3, 4), K2tog, K9 (10, 10), W&T. 3 sts dec.
Row 6: P21 (22, 23), Ssp, P2, Ssp, P3 (3, 4), Ssp, P9 (10, 10), W&T. 3 sts dec.
Row 7: K27 (28, 30), K2tog, K6 (7, 7), W&T. 1 st dec.
Row 8: P23 (24, 26) Ssp, P6 (7, 7), W&T. 1 st dec.
Row 9: K to beginning of rnd.

Transition to Heel Decrease/Short Rows: (K1, K2tog) twice, K1 (1, 2), K2tog, K46 (49, 50), knitting wraps and sts tog. 3 sts dec.

Heel Decrease/Short Rows

Row 1: (K1, K2tog) twice, K1 (1, 2), K2tog, K6, W&T. 3 sts dec.
Row 2: P13 (13, 14), Ssp, P1, Ssp, P1 (1, 2), Ssp, P6, W&T. 3 sts dec.
Row 3: K to 9 (9, 10) sts before end of rnd, knitting wraps and sts tog. Ssk, K1 (1, 2), (Ssk, K1) twice. 3 sts dec.

Sole Rnds, Sizes 8.75 (9.25)"Only

Rnd 1: K to end, knitting wraps and sts tog.
Rnds 2-3: K to end.
Rnd 4: K2tog 3 times, K37 (40), Ssk 3 times, K2tog 3 times, K37 (40), Ssk 3 times. 12 sts dec.

Sole Rnds, Size 9.75" Only

Rnd 1: K to end, knitting wraps and sts tog.
Rnd 2: K6, K2tog, K41, Ssk, K10, K2tog, K41, Ssk, K6. 4 sts dec.
Rnds 3-4: K to end.
Rnd 5: K2tog 3 times, K41, Ssk 3 times, K2tog 3 times, K41, Ssk 3 times. 12 sts dec.

Cut yarn, leaving 36" tail. Divide sts onto two needles, 43 (46, 47) sts each, and use tail to graft sides together using Kitchener Stitch.

Left Slipper

Instep
CO as for Right Slipper.
Instep Setup Rows
Row 1 (WS): Using largest needle and working yarn, P21.
Row 2 (RS): Switch to smallest needles. K2, P17, K2.
Row 3: Sl2, K17, P2.
Row 4: Sl1, K1, P17, K2.
With RS facing, instep will have one Sl st on the right side and two Sl sts on the left.

Main Cable
WS Rows: Sl2, work Main Cable Chart for your size, P2.
RS Rows: Sl1, K1, work Main Cable Chart for your size, K2.
Cont as for Right Slipper.

Toe Cable
WS Rows: Sl2, work Toe Cable Chart, P2.
RS Rows: Sl1, K1, work Toe Cable Chart, K2.
Cont as for Right Slipper.

Toe Finishing

Row 1: Sl1, K1, P1, K2.
Row 2: Work 5-st Decrease as for Right Slipper.
Cut a 12" tail. BO by threading tail through remaining st. Block cabled section of Instep to measurements, inside the Sl st edges.

Sole

Read through entire section carefully before beginning. Remove scrap yarn from CO edge and place sts on smallest needle. Use circular needles to PU but NOT knit one st for each slipped sts along right edge of instep (the edge with only one slipped st). 61 (64, 67) sts on each needle, 122 (128, 134) sts total.

Using largest circular needles and two strands of yarn held together, work Sole Setup Rnd.
Sole Setup Rnd: K slipped sts to 20 sts from end. Place CO edge beneath slipped sts at toe, with RS of CO edge facing up. (Both ends should have the RS facing up, with the tapered end overlapping the CO end. This will form a "teardrop" shape.) For next 20 sts, work in CO edge by knitting each slipped st tog with a CO st TBL. Join in the rnd. K4. PM to mark beginning of rnd.

Next Rnd: K.
Cont as for Right Slipper.

Finishing (both Slippers)

Pin free edge of Instep Toe flat to Instep with sewing pins. Stitch free edge of Instep Toe in place with tail of Instep BO. Cont by stitching free edge of Instep to underside of Instep Toe.
Cut a 15 (16, 17)" length of elastic cord. Using yarn needle, start at the toe end and thread cord elastic through the "tube" created by the two slipped sts on the upper edge of the slipper. Leave a 1" tail at each end of the elastic. (This will gather the threaded sts somewhat.) Stitch each tail to the inside of the toe with sewing needle and thread.
Weave in ends.
Block slippers lightly with sole facing down, such that the sole lays flat. Do not use sock blockers.

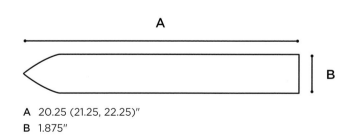

A 20.25 (21.25, 22.25)"
B 1.875"

Legend

K
RS: Knit stitch
WS: Purl stitch

P
RS: Purl stitch
WS: Knit stitch

P2tog
RS: Purl two stitches together.
WS: Knit two stitches together.

P2tog TBL
RS: Purl 2 stitches together in back loops, inserting needle from the left, behind and into the backs of the 2nd and 1st sts, in that order.
WS: Sl 1 st as if to knit, sl another st as if to knit. Insert LH needle into front of these 2 sts and knit them together.

KYOK
K1 and leave on needle. YO, then knit again into the same st to make 3 sts from 1.

No Stitch

Pattern Repeat

2-St Decrease
Sl 3 sts to RH needle. On RH needle, pass adjoining st over LH st. Sl LH st back to LH needle. On LH needle, pass adjoining st over RH st. P remaining st. 2 sts dec.

5-St Decrease
Sl 3 sts to RH needle. *On RH needle, pass 2nd st from needle tip over first and off needle. Sl remaining st back to LH needle. On LH needle, pass 2nd st from needle over 1st st and off needle.* Sl remaining st back to RH needle. Rep from * to *. 4 sts dec.

Left Twist (LT)
RS: Sl1 to CN, hold in front. K1, K1 from CN.
WS: Left Twist

Right Twist (RT)
RS: Skip the 1st st, knit into 2nd st, then knit skipped st. Slip both sts off LH needle.
WS: Skip 1st st, purl into 2nd st, then purl the skipped st.

Left Twist, purl bg
RS: Sl1 to CN, hold in front. P1, K1 from CN.
WS: Left twist purl.

Right Twist, Purl bg
RS: Sl1 to CN, hold in back. K1, P1 from CN.
WS: Right twist purl.

C1 Over 1 Right - Purl bg
Place 2 sts on CN, hold in back, K1. Move center st from CN back to LH needle and purl it. K1 from CN.

C1 Over 1 Left - Purl f/bg
Place 2 sts on CN, bring to front, P1. Move 1 st from CN to LH needle. Move CN to back between LH and RH needles. K1 from LH needle. P1 from CN.

Main Cable Chart 8.75"

Main Cable Chart 9.25"

Main Cable Chart 9.75"

Toe Cable Chart

| 23 | 22 | 21 | 20 | 19 | 18 | 17 | 16 | 15 | 14 | 13 | 12 | 11 | 10 | 9 | 8 | 7 | 6 | 5 | 4 | 3 | 2 | 1 |

Rows (right side, bottom to top): 1, 2, 3, 4, 5, 6, 7, 8, 9, 10, 11, 12, 13, 14, 15, 16, 17, 18, 19, 20, 21, 22, 23, 24, 25, 26, 27, 28, 29

MIXIT HAT

by Lena Mathisson

FINISHED MEASUREMENTS

18.5" circumference x 7.5" high.

YARN

Knit Picks Stroll Sock Yarn
(75% Superwash Merino Wool, 25%
Nylon): MC Midnight Heather 24592, 1
ball; C1 Cobblestone Heather 27236, C2
Dusk 23693, C3 Sprinkle Heather 24595,
C4 Duchess Heather 24594, 1 ball each,
or 15 - 30 yards each of 4 contrast colors.
A different number of contrast colors can
be used; adjust yarn amounts accordingly.

NEEDLES

US 3 (3.25 mm) 16" circular needle and
DPNs, or size to obtain gauge.

NOTIONS

Yarn Needle
Stitch Markers

GAUGE

30 sts and 42 rows = 4" in Broken Seed
Stitch in the rnd, blocked.

For pattern support, contact
hmathisson@optonline.net

Notes:

After finishing socks, shawls, or other projects, you almost always wind up with a little ball of yarn left over. Use that leftover sock/ fingering yarn to make this simple but fun hat. With one main color overlying the contrast stripes, you can create a gentle color gradient or get wild with strong stripes of contrast color.

You only need to be able to knit and purl in order to knit this fun hat, so it's a great project even for a beginner, and a quick knit for someone more experienced.

Seeded Rib (worked in the rnd over multiples of 4 sts)
Rnd 1: *K3, P1, rep from * to end of rnd.
Rnd 2: P1, *K1, P3, rep from * until 3 sts before end of rnd, K1, P2.
Rep Rnds 1-2 for pattern.

DIRECTIONS

Seeded Rib Border

Using first CC, loosely CO 140 sts. Join in the rnd, being careful not to twist sts.* PM for beginning of rnd; SM throughout.
Change to MC, work in Seeded Rib for 1.5" from CO edge.

*Do you just hate that line, "Join in the rnd, being careful not to twist sts"? If you want to work the first few rows flat and close them with a small seam at the end, to make sure you start without twisting, there are instructions in the Finishing section for this.

Body of Hat

Begin working in Broken Seed Stitch. The Broken Seed Stitch pattern consists of 4 rnds, of which 2 are worked in the MC and 2 in the CC. Each CC will be used during two reps of the 4-rnd sequence before switching to the next CC. You will work a total of 56 rnds in this section, which is 14 reps of the 4-rnd Broken Seed Stitch, making 7 colored stripes, before beginning the crown shaping. Use the Stripe Worksheet to plan and keep track of the sequence of CCs that you will use. The Stripe Worksheet includes the 7 stripes for the body of the hat, plus the 2 stripes that you will work as you shape the crown of the hat.

Broken Seed Stitch

Rnd 1: With MC, K.
Rnd 2: With CC, *K1, P1, rep from * to end of rnd.
Rnd 3: With MC, K.
Rnd 4: With CC, *P1, K1, rep from * to end of rnd.
Rep Rnds 1-4 for pattern.

Crown Shaping

Once you have completed the 7 stripes (56 rnds) of Broken Seed Stitch, you are ready to begin the decreases for shaping the crown of the hat.

In the crown section (top of the hat), stitch markers are used to divide the sts into 7 sections, with decreases worked at the beginning and end of each section. The central area of each section will be worked in Broken Seed Stitch, but the dec sts will all be worked in the MC, creating accent lines where the decreases are worked (see picture of crown of hat).

Using the MC during CC rnds requires carrying the main color behind the work on these rnds. For tips on this technique, see the Knit Picks tutorial on stranded knitting at:
http://tutorials.knitpicks.com/fair-isle-or-stranded-knitting/

Change to the next CC in your sequence and re-set your row counter for the crown dec rnds. As the number of sts decreases, at some point it will become more comfortable to switch to DPN's, or employ the Magic Loop method. For a tutorial on this, see:
http://tutorials.knitpicks.com/magic-loop/.

Crown Rnd 1: With MC, *K20, PM, rep from * to end of rnd. You do not need to place a new M at the end of the final rep; your beginning of rnd M will serve for that M. You now have 7 sections marked off, each with 20 sts.
Crown Rnd 2: *With MC, Ssk; with CC, (K1, P1) until 2 sts remain before M; with MC, K2tog, SM; rep from * to end of rnd. 14 sts dec.
Crown Rnds 3 - 8: Rep Crown Rnds 1-2 three times. SMs as you come to them, since you have already placed the Ms ud. 42 sts dec.
After working Crown Rnds 1 – 8, 84 sts remain.
Change to the next CC and work Crown Rnds 1 - 8 again. 28 sts, 4 sts in each section.

Next Rnd: Remove all stitch markers except beginning of rnd M during this rnd. With MC, *Ssk, K2tog, rep from * to end of rnd. 14 sts.
Next Rnd: With MC, *K2tog, rep from * to end of rnd. 7 sts.

Finishing

Break yarn, leaving 8" tail. Use yarn needle to thread through remaining sts, pull tight, tie knot to secure, and weave in ends. Wash and block to Finished Measurements.

Alternate instructions for the first few rows: For those who want to ensure that there is no risk of twisting the CO, CO 140 sts using straight or circular needles, but not DPN's, so that you can work these first few rows flat.

Row 1 (RS): *K3, P1, rep from * to end of row.

Row 2 (WS): K2, *P1, K3, rep from * until 2 sts remain, P1, K1.

Rows 3-4: Rep Rows 1-2.

Row 5: Rep Row 1. If you have been using straight needles, change to either a circular needle or DPN's. At the end of this row, your sts should all be on a circular needle or distributed on DPN's.

PM for beginning of rnd. Making sure that sts are straight and knitted fabric is all hanging straight down from your needle(s), join to work in the rnd. Turn to Ribbing section at beginning of instructions, begin Seeded Rib Stitch with Rnd 2, then cont with instructions from there. Once you've worked a few rnds in the rib pattern, you can sew the little seam to close the first few rows.

Stripe Worksheet		
Stripe - Work 2 repeats of Broken Seed Stitch for each stripe	**Color**	**Total rounds worked in Broken Seed Stitch at the end of this stripe**
Body Stripe 1		8
Body Stripe 2		16
Body Stripe 3		24
Body Stripe 4		32
Body Stripe 5		40
Body Stripe 6		48
Body Stripe 7		56
Crown Stripe 1		64
Crown Stripe 2		72

PEEK-A-BOO FINGERLESS MITTS

by Kathy Lewinski

FINISHED MEASUREMENTS

7 (7.5, 8)" circumference not including thumb gusset x 6.75 (7, 7.25)" long.

YARN

Knit Picks Palette

(100% Peruvian Highland Wool; 231 yards/50g): MC Black 23729, C1 Pimento 24246, C2 Raspberry Heather 24247, C3 Kumquat Heather 25088, C4 Canary 25531, 1 ball each; or 22g MC, 6g each C1, C2, 3g each C3, C4.

NEEDLES

US 1 (2.5mm) DPNs, or size to obtain gauge.

NOTIONS

Yarn Needle
3 Stitch Markers
Scrap Yarn or Stitch Holder

GAUGE

32 sts = 4" in Two Color Broken Seed Stitch in the rnd, blocked (row gauge is not important for this project).

For pattern support, contact
jcraftyenough@gmail.com

Notes:

Colors seem to peek through a mesh of black in these quick and easy fingerless mitts. A simple broken seed stitch pattern worked in two colors looks like a complicated colorwork pattern, while it's actually nothing more than knits and purls.

This is a great project for using up scraps. Try a self-striping or handpainted yarn for the CC for different looks.

Two Color Broken Seed Stitch (in the rnd over an even number of sts)
Rnd 1: K with MC.
Rnd 2: (K1, P1) until end of rnd with CC.
Rnd 3: K with MC.
Rnd 4: (P1, K1) until end of rnd with CC.
Rep Rnds 1-4 for pattern.

K1, P1 Ribbing (in the rnd over an even number of sts)
All Rnds: (K1, P1) until end of rnd.

DIRECTIONS

While working the pattern, change the contrasting colors when they have been worked for the following lengths.
C1 – 2".
C2 – 1.5".
C3 – 1 (1.25, 1.25)".
C4 - 0.5 (0.5, 0.75)".

Cuff

CO 56 (60, 64) sts with MC. Divide between 3 DPNs. Join together to knit in the rnd, PM between the last and first sts to mark rnds.
Work in K1, P1 Ribbing for 1".
Work in Two Color Broken Seed Stitch with MC and C1 for 1" ending on Rnd 4 of the stitch pattern,

Hand and Thumb Gusset

Rnd 1: K28 (30, 32), PM, M1, PM, K28 (30, 32). 57 (61, 65) sts.
Rnd 2: (K1, P1) 14 (15, 16) times, SM, P1, SM, (K1, P1) 14 (15, 16) times.

Rnd 3: K28 (30, 32), SM, M1L, K1, M1R, SM, K28 (30, 32). 59 (63, 67) sts.
Rnd 4: (P1, K1) 14 (15, 16) times, SM, P1, K1, P1, SM, (P1, K1) 14 (15, 16) times.
Rnd 5: K28 (30, 32), SM, M1L, K to M, M1R, SM, K28 (30, 32). 61 (65, 69) sts.
Rnd 6: (K1, P1) 14 (15, 16) times, SM, P1, (K1, P1) to M, SM, (K1, P1) 14 (15, 16) times.
Rnd 7: K28 (30, 32), SM, M1L, K to M, M1R, SM, K28 (30, 32). 63 (67, 71) sts.
Rnd 8: (P1, K1) 14 (15, 16), times SM, P1, (K1, P1) to M, SM, (P1, K1) 14 (15, 16) times.
Cont working Rnds 5 – 8, increasing 2 sts between the thumb gusset stitch markers on every odd rnd until there are 21 (21, 23) gusset sts between the stitch markers. 77 (81, 87) sts.

Work without increasing between the markers until the thumb gusset is 2.25 (2.5, 2.75)" long. End on an even rnd.
Next Rnd: K28 (30, 32), place 21 (21, 23) sts on scrap yarn or stitch holder for the thumb, K28 (30, 32). 56 (60, 64) sts.
Continue working in Two Color Broken Seed Stitch for 2" ending on an odd rnd. Break CC.
Work K1, P1 Ribbing for 0.5" in MC.
BO in pattern.

Thumb

Put the 21 (21, 23) held thumb sts on 3 DPNs to work in the rnd.
With MC, K until end of rnd, PU and K 1 st from the hand, PM. 22 (22, 24) sts.
Work in Two Color Broken Seed Stitch with MC and CC to match the same place on the hand for about 0.25". End on a K rnd. Break CC.
Work in K1, P1 Ribbing for 0.5" in MC.
BO in pattern.

Finishing

Weave in ends, wash and block.

ROWS OF CANDY SHAWL

by Heike Campbell

FINISHED MEASUREMENTS
19" deep x 65" wingspan.

YARN

Knit Picks Palette
(100% Peruvian Highland Wool; 231 yards/50g): MC White (MC) 23728, 3 balls; C1 Seraphim 26037; C2 Comfrey 26050; C3 Mineral Heather 25546; C4 Indigo Heather 26051, 1 ball each.

NEEDLES
US 6 (4mm) straight or circular needles, or size to obtain gauge.

NOTIONS
Yarn Needle
Removable Stitch Marker, or Scrap Yarn

GAUGE
22 sts and 32 rows = 4" over Garter st, blocked.

19 sts and 36 rows = 4" in Candy Pattern, blocked.

16 sts and 28 rows = 4" in Wrapper Pattern, blocked.

Gauge is not critical for this item; however, it will affect the overall size of the shawl and amount of yarn used.

For pattern support, contact
heikicampbell@gmail.com

Notes:

Rows of Candy is a crescent-shaped shawl with a colorful, unusual border pattern resembling rows of yummy, brightly colored candy – irresistible and ideal to use up leftover yarns.

The shawl is worked from the top down with 3 edge stitches at the beginning and end of each row. The edge stitches are worked in Garter stitch (knit on RS and WS) and the first stitch should be slipped purlwise to create a neat edge. The main body of the shawl is worked in Garter stitch and every pair of right and wrong side rows adds six stitches to the stitch count. The shawl border is worked straight, without any increases to the stitch count other than within the stitch patterns. It starts with the Candy Pattern, an unusual slip stitch and nupps color pattern, where the nupps are framed with crossed, elongated slip stitches. Only one color is worked in each row. The border is finished with a simple candy wrapper eyelet lace pattern and a 2-color stretchy bind off.

The Candy Pattern and Wrapper Pattern are given in form of charts and as fully written instructions. They do not contain the edge stitches. When working from the charts, follow RS rows (odd numbers) from right to left, and WS rows (even numbers) from left to right.

Candy Pattern (worked flat over variable sts)
Do not break MC throughout; carry it up along the side of your work.

Row 1 (RS): With MC, knit.
Row 2 (WS): With MC, P1, *P1 elongated, P2, P1 elongated, P1; rep from * to end.
Row 3: With CC, K1, SL1 WYIB and drop extra wrap, K2, SL1 WYIB and drop extra wrap, *(K1, YO, K1, YO, K1) all in one st, SL1 WYIB and drop extra wrap K2, SL1 WYIB and drop extra wrap; rep from * to last st, K1.
Row 4: With CC, P1, *SL1 WYIF, P2, SL1 WYIF, K5; rep from * to last 5 sts, SL1 WYIF, P2, SL1 WYIF, P1.
Row 5: With CC, K1, SL1 WYIB, K2, SL1 WYIB, *P5, SL1 WYIB, K2, SL1 WYIB; rep from * to last st, K1.
Row 6: With CC, P1, *SL1 WYIF, P2, SL1 WYIF, K2tog, K3tog, pass the 2nd st on RH needle over first st; rep from * to last 5 sts, SL1 WYIF, P2, SL1 WYIF, P1.
Break CC and carry MC up the side of work.
Row 7: With MC, K1, Cross 4, *K1, Cross 4; rep from * to last st, K1.
Row 8: With MC, Purl.

Wrapper Pattern (worked flat over multiples of 19 sts)
Row 1 (RS): K2, YO, SSK, K11, K2tog, YO, K2.
Row 2 and all other WS Rows through Row 14: Purl.
Row 3: K3, YO, SSK, K1, K2tog, YO, K1, (YO, SSK) twice, K1, K2tog, YO, K3.
Row 5: K4, YO, Sk2p, YO, K5, YO, Sk2p, YO, K4.
Row 7: K4, K2tog, YO, K7, YO, SSK, K4.
Row 9: K3, K2tog, YO, K1, YO, SSK, K3, K2tog, YO, K1, YO, SSK, K3.

Row 11: K2, K2tog, YO, K3, YO, SSK, YO, Sk2p, YO, K3, YO, SSK, K2.

Row 13: K1, K2tog, YO, K13, YO, SSK, K1.

2-color Stretchy Bind Off: *With C1 K2togTBL, SL st just made from RH needle back onto LH needle, with C2 K2togTBL, SL st just made from RH needle back onto LH needle; rep from * to end

SL1: SL1 P-wise.

P1 Elongated: Insert tip of RH needle into first st on LH needle as if to purl, wrap yarn twice around tip of RH needle and purl.

Cross 4: Drop first elongated st on LH needle and let hang in front of work, SL the next 2 sts on LH needle onto RH needle, drop 2nd elongated st and let hang in front of work, insert LH needle into first dropped st, SL the 2 sts from RH needle back onto LH needle and insert LH needle into 2nd dropped st, then K4.

KYOK- (K1, YO, K1): Worked in 1 st: K1, leave on needle, YO, then knit again into same st to make 3 sts from 1. 2 sts inc.

DIRECTIONS

Garter Tab

With MC and using the long-tail method, CO 3 sts.
Knit 8 rows; do not turn work after last row. Rotate work 90 degrees, PU and K 4 sts from selvedge edge (1 st for each garter stitch ridge), then PU and K 3 sts from CO edge. 10 sts.

Next Row (WS): SL1P-wise, K to end.
Turn work and insert a removable marker or scrap yarn into second st in the row below to mark the RS of the shawl.

Shawl Body

Row 1 (RS): With MC, SL1 P-wise, K2, YO, K to last 3 sts, YO, K3. 2 sts inc. 12 sts.

Row 2 (WS): SL1 P-wise, K2, KYOK, K to last 4 sts, KYOK, K3. 4 sts inc. 16 sts.

Rep Rows 1 and 2 until you have 268 sts, ending after a WS row (Row 86).
Do not break MC throughout, carry it up the side of your work.

Join C1 and work 4 more rows in Garter stitch, increasing sts at the beginning and end of rows as established. 280 sts.
Break C1 and cont with MC.

Next Row (RS): With MC, SL1 P-wise, K2, YO, K to last 3 sts, YO, K3. 282 sts.

Next Row (WS): SL1 P-wise, K2, KYOK, P to last 4 sts, KYOK, K3. 286 sts.

Shawl Border

The shawl border is worked straight without any further increases other than within the Candy Pattern as explained. Each RS row begins with the 3 edge sts, followed by YO, SSK and ends with K2tog, YO, and the 3 edge sts.

Work the 8 rows of Candy Pattern using C2 as CC as follows:

Row 1 (RS): With MC, SL1 P-wise, K2, YO, SSK, work Row 1 of Candy Pattern, working the pattern rep 54 times in total, K2tog, YO, K3. 286 sts.

Row 2: SL1 P-wise, K2, P2, work Row 2 of Candy Pattern, working the pattern rep 54 times in total, P2, K3.

Work the remaining 6 rows of Candy Pattern as established.
Break CC.

Rep Candy Pattern 3 more times, using first C3, then C4 and then C1 as CC.

Cont with MC and work 2 rows in St st as follows:
Next Row (RS): With MC, SL1 P-wise, K2, YO, SSK, K to last 5 sts, K2tog, YO, K3.
Next Row: SL1 P-wise, K2, P to last 3 sts, K3.

Join C2 and work 4 rows in Garter st as follows:
Row 1 (RS): With C2, Sl1 P-wise, K2, YO, SSK, K to last 5 sts, K2tog, YO, K3.
Row 2: Sl1 P-wise, K2, K to last 3 sts, K3.

Rep Rows 1 and 2 once more. Break C2.

Work 2 more rows in St st using MC as follows:
Next Row (RS): With MC, SL1 P-wise, K2, YO, SSK, K to last 5 sts, K2tog, YO, K3.
Next Row: SL1 P-wise, K2, P to last 3 sts, K3.

Continuing with MC, work the 14 rows of Wrapper Pattern as follows:
Row 1 (RS): SL1 P-wise, K2, YO, SSK, K5, work Row 1 of Wrapper Pattern, working the pattern rep 14 times in total, K5, K2tog, YO, K3. 286 sts.
Row 2: SL1 P-wise, K2, P7, work Row 2 of Wrapper Pattern, working the pattern rep 14 times in total, P7, K3.
Work the remaining 12 rows of Wrapper Pattern as established. Break MC.

Bind-Off
Loosely BO all sts using the 2-colour Stretchy Bind Off with C1 and C2. Remember that the yarn has to stretch across the previous BO st and avoid pulling the yarn tightly.

Finishing
Remove marker, weave in ends, wash, block and enjoy.

Legend

K
RS: Knit stitch
WS: Purl stitch

P
RS: Purl stitch
WS: Knit stitch

YO
Yarn Over

Slip Stitch (sl)
RS: Slip stitch as if to purl with yarn in back.
WS: Slip stitch as if to knit with yarn in front.

K2tog
Knit 2 stitches together as 1 stitch.

SSK
Slip 1 stitch as if to knit. Slip another stitch as if to knit. Insert LH needle into front of these 2 stitches and knit them together.

Make 5 Sts in 1 (M5)
(K1, YO, K1, YO, K1) into 1 stitch.

K5tog
K3 tog, K2tog, pass the 2nd st on RH needle over 1st st.

sl1 K2tog PSSO (SK2P)
Slip 1 stitch. K2tog then pass the slipped stitch over.

P1 Elongated
Purl 1 st wrapping yarn twice.

Pattern Repeat

No Stitch

Cross 4
Drop 1st elongated st on LH needle and let hang in front of work. Slip next 2 sts from LH needle onto RH needle. Drop 2nd elongated st and let hang in front of work. Insert LH needle into 1st dropped st, slip the 2 sts from RH needle back onto LH needle, and insert LH needle into 2nd dropped st, then K4.

Candy Pattern Chart

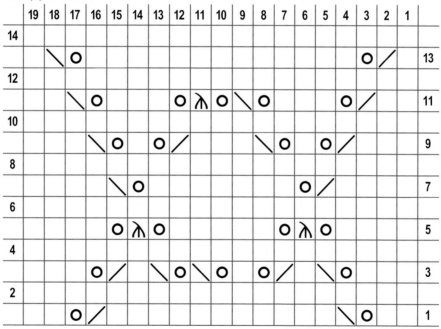

Wrapper Chart

SAMPLER SOCKS

by Meredith Wills

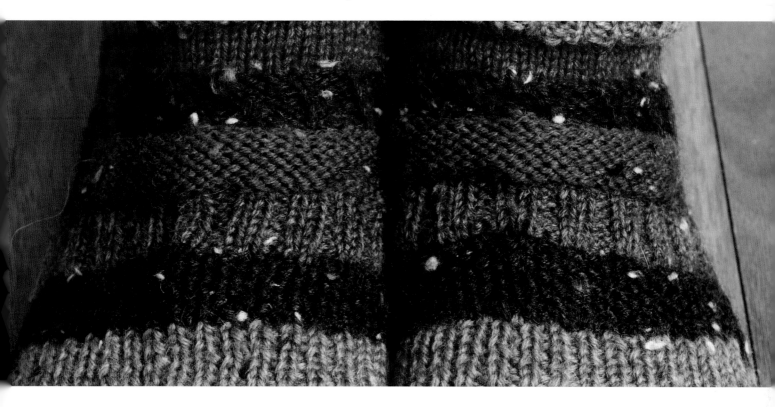

FINISHED MEASUREMENTS

7 (7.75, 9)" foot and leg circumference; sock is meant to be worn with slight negative ease.

YARN

Knit Picks Stroll Tweed
(65% Fine Superwash Merino Wool, 25% Nylon, 10% Donegal Tweed; 231 yards/50g): MC Persimmon Tweed 27233, C1 Firecracker Heather 26288, C2 Garnet Heather 26283, C3 Marine Heather 26290, C4 Forest Heather 26298, C5 Sequoia Heather 26293; 1 ball each, or approximately 25g of MC and 15g each CC.

NEEDLES

US 0 (2mm) DPNs and one 24" circular needle, or one size smaller than size to obtain gauge.

US 1 (2.25mm) DPNs, or two 24" circular needles for two circulars technique, or one 32" or longer circular needle for Magic Loop technique, or size to obtain gauge.

NOTIONS

Small Cable Needle
Stitch Markers
Scrap Yarn or Stitch Holder
Yarn Needle

GAUGE

37 sts and 50 rows = 4" in St st in the round on larger needles, blocked.

For pattern support, contact
meredith.j.wills@gmail.com

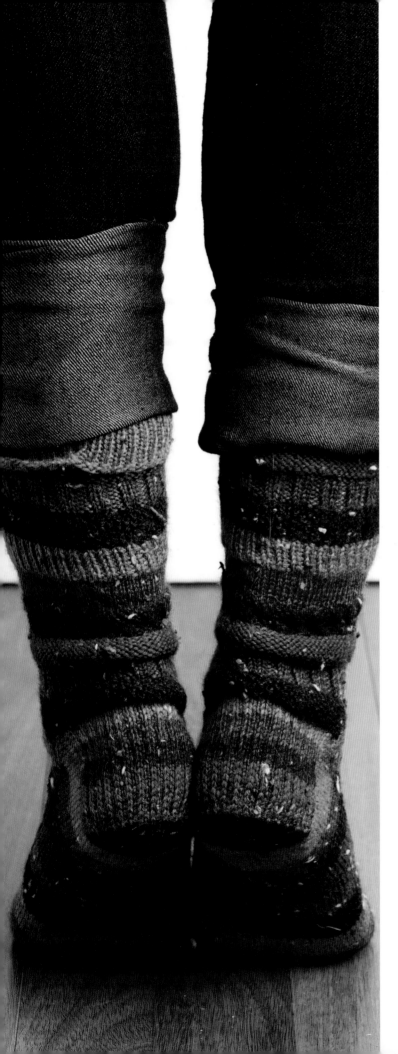

Notes:

This stashbuster project is perfect for those of us who knit a lot of socks. Think of the number of times you've ended up with a partial skein—just enough leftover yarn that you don't want to get rid of it, but not enough for another project. Fortunately, such "orphan ends" are perfect for our Sampler Socks.

Worked in six colors, this pattern incorporates different textures and patterns into each jogless stripe. Not only that, but because the instep and the sole are worked flat and separately, repairs become easy; rather than darning a worn-out heel, you can just frog the area and knit an entirely new section. (See? Yet another use for those "orphan ends"!)

Diagonal Rib (worked in the rnd over multiples of 4 sts)
Rnd 1: K1, P3.
Rnd 2: LC, P2.
Rnd 3: P1, K1, P2.
Rnd 4: P1, LC, P1.
Rnd 5: P2, K1, P1.
Rnd 6: P2, LC.
Rnd 7: P3, K1.

Flat Diagonal Rib (worked flat over multiples of 4 sts; begin with a WS row)
Row 1 (WS): K3, P1.
Row 2 (RS): LC, P2.
Row 3: K2, P1, K1.
Row 4: P1, LC, P1.
Row 5: K1, P1, K2.
Row 6: P2, LC.
Row 7: P1, K3.

Seed Stitch (worked in the rnd over an odd number of sts)
Rnd 1: *K1, P1* rep to 1 st from end of rnd. K1.
Rnd 2: *P1, K1* rep to 1 st from end of rnd. P1.
Rep Rnds 1-2 for pattern.

Instep Seed Stitch (worked flat over an even number of sts)
Row 1: Sl1, *K1, P1* rep to 1 st from end. K1.
Row 2: Sl1, *P1, K1* rep to 1 st from end. P1.
Rep Rows 1-2 for pattern.

1x1 Rib (worked in the rnd over an even number of sts):
All Rnds: *K1, P1* rep to end of rnd.

2x2 Rib (worked in the rnd over multiples of 4 sts):
All Rnds: *K2, P2* rep to end of rnd.

Flat 2x2 Rib (worked flat over multiples of 4 sts plus 2):
Row 1 (WS): Sl1, *P1, K2, P1* rep to 1 st from end. P1.
Row 2 (RS): Sl1, *K1, P2, K1* rep to 1 st from end. K1.
Rep Rows 1-2 for pattern.

Flat 1x1 Rib (worked flat over an even number of sts):
All Rows: Sl1, *K1, P1* rep to 1 st from end. K1.

Left Cable (LC): Sl 1 st onto CN and hold in front, P1, K1 from CN.

Left Twist (LT): Sl 1 st onto CN and hold in front, K1, K1 from CN.

Jogless Stripe: Knit 1 rnd in the new yarn color. Before beginning the 2nd rnd, lift the st below the first st on the LH needle onto the LH needle. Knit the lifted st tog with the first st on the LH needle. Cont stripe as established.

Kitchener Stitch: Follow the instructions provided on the Knit Picks website here:
http://tutorials.knitpicks.com/wptutorials/kitchener-stitch/

DIRECTIONS

Cuff
Until otherwise noted, the pattern is worked on larger needles.
Using MC, loosely CO 64 (72, 84) sts. Join in the rnd. PM to mark beginning of rnd.
Work 1x1 Rib for 1.25".
Cut MC, leaving a 6" tail.

Leg
The leg is worked in the round. Each stripe has 8 rnds except for Leg Stripe 5, which has 10.

Leg Stripe 1
Join C1. K 1 rnd. Begin next rnd with Jogless Stripe, then K 7 rnds. Cut C1, leaving a 6" tail.

Leg Stripe 2
Join C2. K 1 rnd. Begin next rnd with Jogless Stripe. P3, then rep Rnd 1 of Diagonal Rib to end of rnd. Work Rnds 2-7 of Diagonal Rib. Cut C2, leaving a 6" tail.

Leg Stripe 3
Join C3.
Setup Rnd: K1, *K2, LT* rep to 3 sts from end of rnd. K2. Sl final st onto CN, hold in front. Remove M. K first st of next rnd. PM to mark beginning of rnd. K st from CN.
P to end of rnd, then P 6 rnds. Cut C3, leaving a 6" tail.

Leg Stripe 4
Join C4. K 1 rnd. Begin next rnd with Jogless Stripe. K1, P2, then work 2x2 Rib for 7 rnds. Cut C4, leaving a 6" tail.

Leg Stripe 5
Join C5. K to one st from end of rnd, M1L, K1. Begin next rnd with Jogless Stripe. P1, then work Seed Stitch for 9 rnds. Cut C5, leaving a 6" tail. 65 (73, 85) sts.

Leg Stripe 6
Join MC.

Setup Rnd: K1, Ssk, K to end of rnd. 64 (72, 84) sts.
Begin next rnd with Jogless Stripe. P1, then work 1x1 Rib for 7 rnds. Cut MC, leaving a 6" tail.
Rep Leg Stripes 1-5. 65 (73, 85) sts.

Instep
The instep is worked flat, and the first st of each row is a slipped st. Each stripe has 8 rows except for Instep Stripe 5, which has 10.
If desired, the Right and Left Socks can be worked differently from this point, so that the Jogless Stripe sts appear on the inner side of each sock.
Right Sock: Place first 30 (34, 40) sts of rnd on stitch holder. Using MC, K1, Ssk, K to end. 34 (38, 44) instep sts.
Left Sock: Using MC, K1, Ssk, K32 (36, 42). Place remaining sts on stitch holder. 34 (38, 44) instep sts.
Both Socks: Begin working flat. Work 7 rows of Flat 1x1 Rib. Cut MC, leaving a 6" tail.

Instep Stripe 1
Sl1, join C1, K to end. Work 7 rows of St st, slipping first st of each row. Cut C1, leaving a 6" tail.

Instep Stripe 2
Sl1, join C2, K to end. Staring with a WS row, work Instep Diagonal Rib for 7 rows.
Instep Diagonal Rib: Sl1, rep appropriate row of Flat Diagonal Rib to 1 st from end, K1.
Cut C2, leaving a 6" tail.

Instep Stripe 3
Setup Row: Sl1, join C3. K1, *K2, LT* rep to 4 sts from end. K4. Work 7 rows of Rev St st, slipping first st of each row. Cut C3, leaving a 6" tail.

Instep Stripe 4
Sl1, join C4, K to end. Starting with a WS row, work Flat 2x2 Rib for 7 rows, ending with Row 1. Cut C4, leaving a 6" tail.

Instep Stripe 5
Sl1, join C5, K to end. Work Instep Seed Stitch for 9 rows. Cut C5, leaving a 6" tail.

Instep Stripe 6
Sl1, join MC, K to end. Starting with a WS row, work Flat 1x1 Rib for 7 rows, ending with Row 1. Cut MC, leaving a 6" tail.
Rep Instep Stripes 1 (1-2, 1-3).

Instep Toe
The instep toe is worked flat, and the first st of each row is a slipped st.
Switch to smaller needles.
Instep Toe Stripe 1
Sizes 7 (9)" Only, Setup Row (RS): Sl1, join C2 (C4), K to end.
Size 7.75" Only, Setup Row (RS): Sl1, join C3. K1, *K2, LT* rep to 4 sts from end. K4.

All Sizes, Rev St st Toe Ridge (WS): Sl1, K to end.

Instep Toe Decrease
Row 1 (RS): Sl1, Ssk, K to end. 1 st dec.
Row 2 (WS): Sl1, P2tog, P to end. 1 st dec.
Work Instep Toe Decrease Rows 1-2 for 8 (8, 10) rows. 26 (30, 34) instep sts. Cut C2 (C3, C4), leaving a 6" tail.

Instep Toe Stripe 2
Setup Row (RS): Sl1, join C3 (C4, C5), Ssk, K to end.
Starting with Row 2, work Instep Toe Decrease Rows 2-1 for 7 (7, 9) rows. 18 (22, 24) instep sts. Cut C3 (C4, C5), leaving a 6" tail.

Instep Toe Stripe 3
Setup Row (RS): Sl1, join C4 (C5, MC), Ssk, K to end.
Starting with Row 2, work Instep Toe Decrease Rows 2-1 for 7 (9, 9) rows. Cut C4 (C5, MC), leaving a 6" tail.
Place remaining 10 (12, 14) Instep Toe sts on stitch holder.

Heel
The remainder of the sock is worked on smaller needles.

Heel Flap
The heel flap is worked flat, and the first st of each row is a slipped st. PU the 30 (34, 40) sts from stitch holder and work Heel Flap Stripe.

Heel Flap Stripe
Setup Row (RS): Sl1, join MC, *K1, Sl1* rep to 1 st from end, K1.
Heel Flap Stitch
Row 1 (WS): Sl1, P to end.
Row 2 (RS): Sl1, *K1, Sl1* rep to 1 st from end, K1.
Starting with a WS row, work Heel Flap Stitch Rows 1-2 for 7 rows, ending with Row 1.
Cut MC, leaving a 6" tail.
Rep Heel Flap Stripe 4 more times, substituting C1-C4 for each stripe, respectively.

Heel Turn
Row 1 (RS): Sl12 (14, 16), join C5, K5 (5, 7), Ssk, K1. 1 st dec. Turn.
Row 2 (WS): Sl1, P5 (5, 7), P2tog, P1. 1 st dec. Turn.
Row 3: Sl1, K to 1 st before color change, Ssk (working two colors together), K1. 1 st dec. Turn.
Row 4: Sl1, P to 1 st before color change, P2tog (working two colors together), P1. 1 st dec. Turn.
Rep Rows 3 and 4 until all heel flap sts have been worked, ending with a WS row. Cut C5, leaving a 6" tail. 18 (20, 24) heel sts.

Sole
The sole is worked flat, and the first st of each row is a slipped st.
Using DPNs, PU same number of slipped sts from each side of heel flap—approximately 20 sts on each DPN. If desired, PU 1 extra st each side at Instep edge. (This eliminates a possible hole at the join between the Instep and the Sole.) If necessary, place heel sts on DPN. *At the same time* use smaller circular needle to PU slipped sts along each edge of Instep, starting at Toe and picking up same number of sts

each side. (Note: some C5 sts may be included in picked-up sts.) 46 (51, 57) edge sts each side.

Gusset
Row 1 (RS): Sl1, join MC, K heel flap side sts TBL, K heel sts, K heel flap side sts to 1 st from end of Sole sts. PM. Sl final st K-wise to RH needle, then Sl st to circular needle. K Sole st with slipped Instep st together TBL. Turn.
Row 2 (WS): Sl1, P to 1 st from end of Sole sts. PM. Sl final st to RH needle, then Sl st to circular needle. P Sole st together with slipped Instep st. Turn.
Row 3: Sl1, Ssk, K to M, SM. Sl final st K-wise to RH needle, then Sl st to circular needle. K Sole st with slipped Instep st together TBL. Turn.
Row 4: Sl1, P2tog, P to M, SM. Sl final st to RH needle, then Sl st to circular needle. P Sole st together with slipped Instep st. Turn.
Rep Rows 3 and 4 until all MC slipped Instep sts are joined. Cut MC, leaving a 6" tail.
Row 5: Sl1, join C1, Ssk, K to M, SM. Sl final st K-wise to RH needle, then Sl st to circular needle. K Sole st with slipped Instep st together TBL. Turn.
Row 6: Rep Row 4.
Row 7: Rep Row 3.
Rep Rows 6 and 7 until all C1 slipped Instep sts are joined, ending with Row 6. Cut C1, leaving a 6" tail.
Rep Rows 5-7 as established, joining new yarn after first slipped st as needed, until 34 (38, 44) Sole sts remain. If still in the middle of a stripe, do not cut yarn.

Foot
Row 1 (RS): Sl1, K to M, SM. Sl final st K-wise to RH needle, then Sl st to circular needle. K Sole st with slipped Instep st together TBL. Turn.
Row 2 (WS): Sl1, P to M, SM. Sl final st to RH needle, then Sl st to circular needle. P Sole st together with slipped Instep st. Turn.
Rep Rows 1 and 2 as established, joining new yarn after first slipped st as needed, until 12 (13, 15) slipped Instep sts remain.

Sole Toe
Sole Toe Decrease
Row 1 (RS): Rep Gusset Row 3.
Row 2 (WS): Rep Gusset Row 4.
Rep Rows 1 and 2 as established, joining new yarn after first slipped st as needed, until all slipped Instep sts have been joined. Cut final yarn, leaving a 12" tail.
If needed, place remaining 10 (12, 14) Sole Toe sts on DPN. Place Instep Toe sts on a second DPN. Graft toe using Kitchener Stitch.

Finishing
Weave in Leg ends, adjusting tension at joins so stripes appear jogless. Weave in Instep and Sole ends, pulling sts tight so no holes appear along the side of the foot. Weave in remaining ends.

SIMPLICITY SQUARED HAT AND MITTS

by Lisa K. Ross

FINISHED MEASUREMENTS

Hat: 19.5 (20.75, 22.25)" circumference x 8" deep; to be worn with 2-3" negative ease.

Mitts: 6.25 (7, 7.75, 8.25)" circumference x 11 (11, 11.5, 11.5)" total length; to be worn with 0.5" negative ease.

YARN

Hat:

Knit Picks Swish Worsted
(100% Fine Superwash Merino Wool; 110 yards/50g): MC Dove Heather 25631, 1 ball; C1 White 24662, C2 Highlighter Yellow 26646, C3 Pucker 26639, C4 Electric Blue 26645, C5 Gulfstream 25137, C6 Peapod 25139; 1 ball or 18 yards/8g each.

Mitts:

Knit Picks Swish Worsted
(100% Superwash Merino Wool; 110 yards/50g): MC Dove Heather 25631, 1 (1, 2, 2) balls; C1 White 24662, C2 Highlighter Yellow 26646, C3 Pucker 26639, C4 Electric Blue 26645, C5 Gulfstream 25137, C6 Peapod 25139; 1 ball or 18 yards/8g each.

NEEDLES

Hat: US 6 (4mm) DPNs and 16" circular needles, or size to obtain gauge, and US 3 (3.25mm) 16" circular needles, or 3 sizes smaller than size to obtain gauge.

Mitts: US 6 (4mm) DPNs, or size to obtain gauge, and US 3 (3.25mm) DPNs, or 3 sizes smaller than size to obtain gauge.

NOTIONS

Yarn Needle
Stitch Markers
Scrap Yarn or Stitch Holder
Pompom Maker, optional

GAUGE

23 sts and 48 rnds = 4" over Checkered Slip-Stitch Pattern on larger needles in the rnd, blocked.

Notes:

Perfect for your leftover bits and bobs of worsted weight yarn, the Simplicity Squared Hat and Mitts pair a main color with as many contrast colors as you would like. Although they might appear difficult, these designs are actually quite simple. Using only one color at a time, slipped stitches give the appearance of stranded colorwork to create a checkerboard effect. Both designs begin with 1x1 Ribbing and are worked from bottom to top in the round. Complete the set for a colorfully trendy look this season!

1x1 Ribbing (worked in the rnd over even number of sts)
All Rnds: (K1, P1) to end of rnd.

M1L (Make 1 Left-leaning st): PU the bar between st just worked and next st and place on LH needle as a regular st; K TBL.

M1R (Make 1 Right-leaning st): PU the bar between st just worked and next st and place on LH needle backwards (incorrect st mount). K TFL.

Checkered Slip-Stitch Pattern (worked in the rnd over multiple of 4 sts)
Rnds 1-2: With CC, (K2, SL2) to end of rnd.
Rnd 3: With MC, K.
Rnds 4-5: With CC, (SL2, K2) to end of rnd.
Rnd 6: With MC, K.
Rep Rnds 1-6 for pattern.

DIRECTIONS

Hat

Brim
Using smaller needles and MC, loosely CO 102 (110, 118) sts. PM and join to work in the rnd, being careful not to twist sts. Work 1x1 Ribbing for 1.25 (1, 1.25)".

Body
Switch to larger needles.
Increase Rnd 1: *K 10 (11, 11), M1L; rep from * to last 2 (0, 8) sts, K 2 (0, 8). 112 (120, 128) sts.

Using C1, work 2 reps of Checkered Slip-Stitch Pattern. Break C1.
Using C2, work 2 reps of Checkered Slip-Stitch Pattern. Break C2.
Using C3, work 2 reps of Checkered Slip-Stitch Pattern. Break C3.
Using C4, work 2 reps of Checkered Slip-Stitch Pattern. Break C4.
Using C5, work 2 reps of Checkered Slip-Stitch Pattern. Break C5.

Crown

Switch to DPNs when it becomes necessary.

Rnd 1: Using C6, *(K2, SL2) 4 (5, 4) times, PM; rep from * to end of rnd.

Rnd 2: Using C6, *K2TOG, (SL2, K2) 2 (3, 2) times, SL2, SSK, SL2; rep from * 7 (6, 8) times. 98 (108, 112) sts.

Rnd 3: Using MC, K.

Rnd 4: Using C6, *SL1, (K2, SL2) 2 (3, 2) times, K2, SL3; rep from * to end of rnd.

Rnd 5: Using C6, *K2TOG, K1, (SL2, K2) 1 (2, 1) time(s), SL2, K1, SSK, SL2; rep from * 7 (6, 8) times. 84 (96, 96) sts.

Rnd 6: Using MC, K.

Rnd 7: Using C6, *(SL2, K2) 2 (3, 2) times, SL4; rep from * to end of rnd.

Rnd 8: Using C6, *using tip of right needle, lift 2nd st on left needle over first st, SL1 (K2, SL2) 1 (2, 1) time(s), K2, SL2 K-wise, one at a time, pass first slipped st over second slipped st on right needle, SL2; rep from * 7 (6, 8) times. 70 (84, 80) sts.

Rnd 9: Using MC, K.

Rnd 10: Using C6, *K1, (SL2, K2) 1 (2, 1) time(s), SL2, K1, SL2; rep from * to end of rnd.

Rnd 11: Using C6, *using tip of right needle, lift 2nd st on left needle over first st, SL2, (K2, SL2) 0 (1, 0) time(s), K2, SL1, SL2 K-wise, one at a time, pass first slipped st over second slipped st on right needle, SL2; rep from * 7 (6, 8) times. 56 (72, 64) sts.

Rnd 12: Using MC, K.

Rnd 13: Using C6, (K2, SL2) to end of rnd.

Rnd 14: Using C6, *K2TOG, (SL2, K2) 0 (1, 0) time(s), SL2, SSK, SL2; rep from * 7 (6, 8) times. 42 (60, 48) sts.

Rnd 15: Using MC, K.

Rnd 16: Using C6, *SL1, (K2, SL2) 1 (2, 1) time(s), SL1; rep from * to end of rnd.

Rnd 17: Using C6, *K2TOG, (K1, SL2) 0 (1, 0) time(s), SSK, SL2 (3, 2); rep from * 7 (6, 8) times. 28 (48, 32) sts.

Rnd 18: Using MC, *SL2, (K2TOG, SL2) 0 (1, 0) time(s), K2; rep from * 7 (6, 8) times. 28 (42, 32) sts.

Rnd 19: Using C6, *K2TOG, (SL1, SSK) 0 (1, 0) time(s), SL2; rep from * 7 (6, 8) times. 21 (30, 24) sts.

Size 20.75" ONLY

Rnd 20: Using C6, (K3TOG, SL2) 6 times. 18 sts. Break C6.

Rnd 21: Using MC, (SL1, K2TOG) 6 times. 12 sts.

Rnd 22: Using MC, K2TOG around, removing all Ms. 6 sts.

Sizes 19.5 and 22.25" ONLY, Rnd 20: Break C6. Using MC, K3TOG around, removing all Ms. 7 (-, 8) sts.

All Sizes: Using a yarn needle, pull MC through remaining sts.

Mitts (make 2 the same)

Cuff

Using smaller needles and MC, loosely CO 30 (36, 40, 42) sts. PM and join to work in the rnd, being careful not to twist sts. Work 1x1 Ribbing for 3".

Palm

Switch to larger needles.

Inc Rnd 1: *K 5 (9, 10, 7), M1L; rep from * to end of rnd. 36 (40, 44, 48) sts.

Using C1, work 2 reps of Checkered Slip-Stitch Pattern, then Rnds 1-5 of Checkered Slip-Stitch Pattern. Break C1.

Gusset

Note: When working M1L and M1R increases in this section, be sure to use the MC bar running between the sts instead of the CC.

Set-up Rnd: Using MC, M1R, K2, M1L, PM for gusset, K to end of rnd. 2 gusset sts inc. 38 (42, 46, 50) sts.

Rnds 1-2: Using C2, SL1, K2, SL1, SM, (SL2, K2) to last 2 sts, SL2.

Rnd 3: Using MC, K1, M1R, K2, M1L, K1, SM, K to end of rnd. 40 (44, 48, 52) sts.

Rnds 4-5: Using C2, SL1, K1, SL2, K1, SL1, SM, (K2, SL2) to last 2 sts, K2.

Rnd 6: Using MC, K1, M1R, K to 1 st before M, M1L, K1, SM, K to end of rnd. 2 sts inc. 42 (46, 50, 54) sts.

Rnds 7-8: Using C2, SL3, K2, SL3, SM, (SL2, K2) to last 2 sts, SL2.

Rnd 9: Using MC, Rep Rnd 6. 44 (48, 52, 56) sts.

Rnds 10-11: Using C2, (SL2, K2) twice, SL2, SM, (K2, SL2) to last 2 sts, K2.

Rnd 12: Using MC, Rep Rnd 6. 46 (50, 54, 58) sts.

Rnds 13-14: Using C2, SL1, (K2, SL2) twice, K2, SL1, SM, (SL2, K2) to last 2 sts, SL2.

Rnd 15: Using MC, Rep Rnd 6. 48 (52, 56, 60) sts.

Rnds 16-17: Using C2, SL1, K1, (SL2, K2) twice, SL2, K1, SL1, SM, (K2, SL2) to last 2 sts, K2. Break C2.

Rnd 18: Using MC, Rep Rnd 6. 50 (54, 58, 62) sts.

Rnds 19-20: Using C3, SL3, (K2, SL2) twice, K2, SL3, SM, (SL2, K2) to last 2 sts, SL2.

Rnd 21: Using MC, Rep Rnd 6. 52 (56, 60, 64) sts.

Rnds 22-23: Using C3, SL2, (K2, SL2) 4 times, SM, K2, SL2, (K2, SL2) to last 2 sts, K2.

Using scrap yarn or stitch holder, place the first 18 gusset sts of the rnd on hold, removing the gusset M. 34 (38, 42, 46) sts.

Hand

Set-up Rnd: Using MC, CO 2 sts, K to end of rnd. 36 (40, 44, 48) sts.

Using C3, work 2 reps of Checkered Slip-Stitch Pattern. Break C3.

Using C4, work 3 reps of Checkered Slip-Stitch Pattern. Break C4.

Using C5, work 2 (2, 3, 3) reps of Checkered Slip-Stitch Pattern. Break C5.

Top Shaping

Rnd 1: Using C6, (K2, SL2) to end of rnd.

Rnd 2: Using C6, (K2TOG, SL2) to end of rnd. 27 (30, 33, 36) sts.

Rnd 3: Using MC, K.

Rnd 4: Using C6, (SL1, K2) to end of rnd.

Rnd 5: Using C6, (SL1, K2TOG) to end of rnd. 18 (20, 22, 24) sts.

Rnd 6: Using MC, K.

Rnds 7-8: Using C6, (K1, SL1) to end of rnd. Break C6.

Rnd 9: Using MC, K2TOG to end of rnd. 9 (10, 11, 12) sts.

Rnd 10: K2TOG 4 (5, 5, 6) times, K 1 (0, 1, 0). 5 (5, 6, 6) sts. Break yarn. Using a yarn needle, pull MC through remaining sts.

Thumb

Place 18 held sts onto larger needles.

Set-up Rnd: Using MC, K across sts, PU and K 2 sts, PM and join to work in the rnd. 20 sts.

Using C3, work 2 reps of Checkered Slip-Stitch Pattern. Break C3.

Using C4, work 1 (2, 3, 3) reps of Checkered Slip-Stitch Pattern.

Sizes 7.75 and 8.25" Only: Using C5, work – (-, 1, 2) reps of Checkered Slip-Stitch Pattern.

Thumb Shaping

The remainder of the thumb will be worked using MC and current CC.

Rnd 1: Using CC, (SL2, K2TOG) to end of rnd. 15 sts.

Rnd 2: Using MC, K to end of rnd.

Rnd 3: Using CC, (K2, SL1) to end of rnd.

Rnd 4: Using CC, (K2TOG, SL1) to end of rnd. 10 sts. Break CC.

Rnd 5: Using MC, K to end of rnd.

Rnd 6: K2TOG to end of rnd. 5 sts.

Break yarn. Using a yarn needle, pull MC through remaining sts.

Finishing (Hat and Mitts)

Weave in ends, wash and block to finished measurements. If desired, add a pompom to the blocked hat.

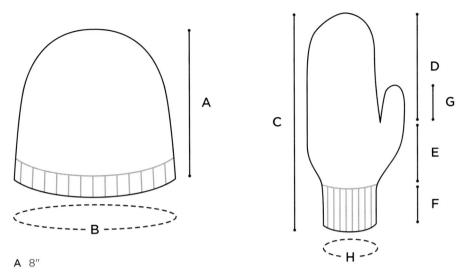

A 8"
B 19.5 (20.75, 22.25)"

C 11 (11, 11.5, 11.5)"
D 4.5 (4.5, 5, 5)"
E 3.5"
F 3"
G 2 (2.25, 2.5, 2.75)"
H 6.25 (7, 7.75, 8.25)"

TELLURIDE SLOUCH HAT

by Jenny Williams

FINISHED MEASUREMENTS

18.25 (20.5, 22.75)" circumference and 10.25" long.

YARN

Knit Picks Wool of the Andes Worsted
(100% Peruvian Highland Wool; 110 yards/50g): MC Dove Heather 24077, C1 Marble Heather 25976, C2 Onyx Heather 24076, 1 ball each.

NEEDLES

US 7 (4.5mm) DPNs or two 24" circular needles for two circulars technique, or one 32" circular needle for Magic Loop technique, or size to obtain gauge.

NOTIONS

Yarn Needle
Stitch Markers

GAUGE

21 sts and 28 rows = 4" in stranded St st in the round, blocked.

For pattern support, contact
jennyw@tcworks.net

Notes:

This hat is a unisex design, ready for anybody to grab and look great on their way out the door! The combination of wool and stranding keeps those precious ears toasty and warm. Worked with worsted weight yarn and just 2 colors at a time, this hat is fast and fun with satisfying results. Proper blocking will give the have a relaxed, slouchy look.

The chart is worked in the rnd; read each row from right to left as a RS row.

Rib Stitch Pattern (in the rnd over an even number of sts)
All Rnds: *K1, P1; rep from * to end of rnd.

M1L (Make 1 Left-leaning st)
Sl the bar between st just worked and next st onto the LH needle, inserting LH needle under the bar from front to back. Knit TBL. The resulting st will be twisted which prevents it from making a hole.

DIRECTIONS
Using C1, loosely CO 86 (98, 110) sts. PM and join to begin working in the rnd, taking care not to twist sts. Work Rib Stitch Pattern for 1.25" from CO edge.
Next Rnd: *Using C1, K1, using C2, P1; rep from * to end of rnd.
Next Rnd: Using only C1, work in Rib Stitch Pattern.

Hat Body
Inc Rnd: Change to MC and *K8 (10, 11), M1L; rep to last 6 (8, 0) sts, M0 (M1, M0). 96 (108, 120) sts.
Work Telluride Slouch Hat Chart 8 (9, 10) times to end of rnd. Work in established pattern through Row 43 of Telluride Slouch Hat Chart. Break CC's.
Using MC, knit 1".
Next Rnd: *K6, PM; rep from * to end of rnd.

Crown Shaping
Rnd 1: *K to 2 sts before M, K2tog, SM; rep from *to end of rnd. 80 (90, 100) sts.
Rnd 2: Knit to end of rnd.
Repeat Rnds 1 – 2 3 more times. 32 (36, 40) sts.
Next Rnd: *K2tog; rep from * to end of rnd, removing markers as you go. 16 (18, 20) sts.
Thread yarn through remaining sts and pull tight.

Finishing
Weave in ends. To relax fibers, immerse in lukewarm water for 15 minutes. Gently press out water, trying not to twist hat. Place hat between towels and step on hat, removing remaining water. For a slouchier look, place hat on a ball similar in size to desired head circumference, i.e. a soccer ball or balloon. Allow to dry thoroughly and enjoy!

Legend

Telluride Slouch Hat Chart

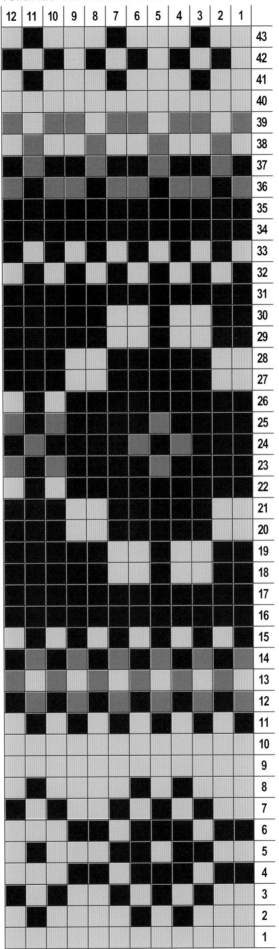

TWISTY POP HAT AND COWL

by Solène Le Roux

FINISHED MEASUREMENTS

Hat: 18.25 (19.5, 20.5, 21.75)"
circumference x 10" high.

Cowl: 25" circumference x 10" high.

YARN

Knit Picks Swish DK
(100% Fine Superwash Merino Wool; 123
yards/50g): C1 White 24064, C2 Honey
26061, 2 balls each.

NEEDLES

US 4 (3.5mm) DPNs and 16" circular
needles for Hat; 24" circular needles or
one 32" or longer circular needle for
Magic Loop technique for Cowl, or size
to obtain gauge.

NOTIONS

Yarn Needle
Stitch Markers

GAUGE

21 sts and 23 rows = 4" over Twisty Pop
Stitch Pattern in the rnd, blocked.

For pattern support, contact
soleneknits@gmail.com

Notes:

This colorblock set is inspired by twisty pop lollipops. It's a great stashbuster and quick project that you can work in two (or more!) colors of Swish DK.

This set is made up of a hat and cowl, both worked in the round with an allover textured pattern made with a bind off stitch and a central yarn over. The color changes are worked as a full knit round to be completely invisible.

When working the chart, read each row from right to left as a RS row.

P3SO: Pass 3rd st on LH needle over first 2 sts and off needle.

Twisty Pop Stitch Pattern (in the rnd over multiples of 6 sts)
Rnd 1: P3SO, K1, YO, K1, P3.
Rnd 2-4: K3, P3.
Rep Rnds 1-4 for pattern.

K1, P1 Rib (in the rnd over an even number of sts)
All Rnds: (K1, P1) to end of rnd.

DIRECTIONS

Hat
Hem
With C1, loosely CO 96 (102, 108, 114) sts. PM for start of rnd, join to work in the rnd, being careful not to twist sts.
Rnds 1-8: Work in K1, P1 Rib.

Body
Begin working Twisty Pop Stitch Pattern.
Work Rnds 1-4 of Twisty Pop Stitch Pattern 4 times.
Rep Rnds 1-2 one more time.
Color Change Rnd: Cut C1, with C2, K to end.
Rep Rnd 4 of Twisty Pop Stitch Pattern.

Work Rnds 1-4 of Twisty Pop Stitch Pattern 5 times.
Rep Rnds 1-2 one more time.

Crown Decreases
Rnd 1: (K1, K2tog, SSK, P1) to end. 64 (68, 72, 76) sts.
Rnd 2: (K3, P1) to end.
Rnd 3: (K2tog, SSK) to end. 32 (34, 36, 38) sts.
Rnd 4: K to end.
Rnd 5: (K2tog) to end. 16 (17, 18, 19) sts.
Rnd 6: K to end.
Rnd 7: (K2tog) to 0 (1, 0, 1) st before end, K0 (1, 0, 1). 8 (9, 9, 10) sts.
Cut yarn, thread it through last 8 (9, 9, 10) sts, pull to fasten off.

Cowl
Hem
With C1, CO 132 sts. PM for start of rnd, join to work in the rnd, being careful not to twist sts.
Rnds 1-8: Work in K1, P1 Rib.

Body
Begin working Twisty Pop Stitch Pattern.
Work Rnds 1-4 of Twisty Pop Stitch Pattern 4 times.
Rep Rnds 1-2 one more time.
Color Change Rnd: Cut C1, with C2, K to end.
Rep Rnd 4 of Twisty Pop Stitch Pattern.
Work Rnds 1-4 of Twisty Pop Stitch Pattern 5 times.
Rep Rnd 1 one more time.

Hem
Rnds 1-8: Work in K1, P1 Rib.
BO in pattern.

Finishing
Weave in ends, wash and block to dimensions.

Twisty Pop Chart

6	5	4	3	2	1	
●	●	●				4
●	●	●				3
●	●	●				2
●	●	●		O		1

Legend

	K
□	Knit stitch

	P
●	Purl stitch

	P3SO
O	Pass 3rd st on LH needle over first 2 sts and off needle.

Abbreviations

BO	bind off	**KFB**	knit into the front and back of stitch
BOR	beginning of round	**K-wise**	knitwise
cn	cable needle	**LH**	left hand
CC	contrast color	**M**	marker
CDD	Centered double dec	**M1**	make one stitch
CO	cast on	**M1L**	make one left-leaning stitch
cont	continue	**M1R**	make one right-leaning stitch
dec	decrease(es)	**MC**	main color
DPN(s)	double pointed needle(s)	**P**	purl
EOR	every other row	**P2tog**	purl 2 sts together
inc	increase	**PM**	place marker
K	knit	**PFB**	purl into the front and back of stitch
K2tog	knit two sts together	**PSSO**	pass slipped stitch over

PU	pick up
P-wise	purlwise
rep	repeat
Rev St st	reverse stockinette stitch
RH	right hand
rnd(s)	round(s)
RS	right side
Sk	skip
Sk2p	sl 1, k2tog, pass slipped stitch over k2tog: 2 sts dec
SKP	sl, k, psso: 1 st dec
SL	slip
SM	slip marker
SSK	sl, sl, k these 2 sts tog

SSP	sl, sl, p these 2 sts tog tbl
SSSK	sl, sl, sl, k these 3 sts tog
St st	stockinette stitch
sts	stitch(es)
TBL	through back loop
TFL	through front loop
tog	together
W&T	wrap & turn (see specific instructions in pattern)
WE	work even
WS	wrong side
WYIB	with yarn in back
WYIF	with yarn in front
YO	yarn over

Knit Picks yarn is both luxe and affordable—a seeming contradiction trounced! But it's not just about the pretty colors; we also care deeply about fiber quality and fair labor practices, leaving you with a gorgeously reliable product you'll turn to time and time again.

THIS COLLECTION FEATURES

Stroll Sock Yarn
Fingering Weight
75% Fine Superwash Merino Wool,
25% Nylon

Stroll Tweed
Fingering Weight
65% Fine Superwash Merino Wool,
25% Nylon, 10% Donegal Tweed

Hawthorne Multi
Fingering Weight
80% Superwash Fine Highland Wool,
20% Polyamind (Nylon)

Wool of the Andes
Worsted Weight
100% Peruvian Highland Wool

Palette
Fingering Weight
100% Peruvian Highland Wool

Andean Treasure
Sport Weight
100% Baby Alpaca

Swish
Worsted & DK Weights
100% Fine Superwash Merino Wool

Alux
Fingering Weight
66% Baby Alpaca,
34% Lurex

Chroma
Fingering Weight
70% Superwash Wool,
30% Nylon

View these beautiful yarns and more at www.Knit Picks.com